Dreaming
of Animals

Dreaming
of Animals

dialogue between self and world

Valerie Harms

MagiCircle PRESS

iUniverse, Inc.
New York Lincoln Shanghai

Dreaming of Animals
dialogue between self and world

Copyright © 2005 by Valerie Harms

iUniverse books may be ordered through booksellers or by contacting:

iUniverse
2021 Pine Lake Road, Suite 100
Lincoln, NE 68512
www.iuniverse.com
1-800-Authors (1-800-288-4677)

Cover design by Rein D. Gillstrom, CDI (Bozeman, MT)
"Egret Moon" art by Rod MacIver/Heron Dance (www.herondance.org).

Contact the author at P.O. Box 1123, Bozeman, MT 5977. See www.valerieharms.com for info about workshops and consulting.

ISBN: 0-595-34311-2

Printed in the United States of America

we are partners in this land,
co-signers of a covenant

—Stanley Kunitz

CONTENTS

INTRODUCTION

THE UNITY OF INNER AND OUTER NATURE

I had a vision of a unified kingdom of animals when I journeyed to the Galapagos Islands, situated 500 miles or so from land in the Pacific Ocean. The animals did not yet have the fear of humans that has become imprinted on animals in the rest of the world. I rested next to a sleeping sea lion and stood within hand-shaking distance of penguins and boobies. I swam amidst clouds of curious fish, who approached me first.

When I lay down next to the sea lion, she looked at me languorously. Our skins were coated with sand. We basked under an immense sky, gentle wind, with the persistent sound of frothing waves. How did she view me? I did not really know but for awhile at least we shared a moment of the gift of life. I took in as much as I could the sheen of her coat, the graceful lines of her form, and her peace.

I knew that in the past these once barren volcanic islands, covered with hard lava, had been found by organisms (seeds, spiderlings) from water and the air and which, despite all challenges, over the eons adapted and formed colonies, native to each island. The endemic cultures were the reason why the islands helped Charles Darwin make his famous observations about the evolution of species approximately 150 years ago.

I was also aware how these island ecosystems were destined for future change as our species plunder the fish and turtles, introduce rats and goats, and batter the coasts with tourist boats.

I had been motivated to write this book by similar threats to animals in the rest of the world. As part of my research for this book I traveled to Hawaii, Mexico, Costa Rica, Ecuador, Bali, Spain, and Morocco, where I'd seen how the animals are treated now, as well as the stuffed ones only visible in museums. In rainforests and near seashores I observed some of the wondrous species that inhabit this world. Everywhere I went, wildlife are threatened, usually by people making insensitive economic decisions.

I hate and fear the threats of extinction to animals, because animals have been vital to us since we existed on this planet. For no matter where we live—whether near desert, mountain, jungle, grassland, tundra, lake, or ocean, we dwell amidst a number of other species populations with invisible dynamic links that originated way before our ancestral family appeared millions of years ago. Our lives depend on the crucial functions animals fulfill for the Earth. In breathing, animals produce and maintain oxygen and other gases in the atmosphere. In eating, some maintain a balance of populations between predators and prey. In defecating, they recycle nutrients and help produce fertile soil. Burrowing, they churn and till the soil. Some help regulate water supplies, some pollinate plants, disperse seeds, and decompose organic wastes. (A large fraction of the U.S. food supply depends on native pollinators). In breeding and evolving, animals broaden the gene pool, making possible more medicines, foods, and other resources essential to all living beings. The larger the genetic diversity, the more possible options we have for the optimum survival on this biosphere.

When I had researched the material for my book, *The National Audubon Society Almanac of the Environment/The Ecology of Everyday Life*, I learned how the most eminent scientists were declaring that a fifth or more of the species of plants and animals could vanish or be doomed to early extinction by the year 2020 unless better efforts were made to save them. Within the next 50 years up to 50% of all species could be gone.[1] A severe warning that the relationship between humans and other animals was wounded.

I also knew from my reading and many psychological groups that people dreamed frequently about animals, often injured, and yet when people talked about the animals in their background—from pets to wolf watching—they became excited with affection and wonder. No amount of environmental red flags seem to affect people so much as when their own

---

1.   Edward O. Wilson, *The Diversity of Life* (Cambridge, MA: The Belknap Press of Harvard University Press, 1992), p. 346.

hearts are stirred. I thus decided to explore how our relationship to animals, both wild and familiar, could be healed for the benefit of our lives and the fate of this Earth.

Ever since humans have lived among other animals, we have had ideas ("day dreams") and sleep dreams about them. According to brain research and modern physics, our thoughts are subtle forms of physical matter and capable of traveling across time and space. Combined with emotion and intent, they gain the power to shape events. Our fantasies, feelings, and images have influenced our behavior, and because we project them, they have consequences for our inner and outer worlds. We impact the biosphere's physical resources and consciousness through destructive as well as restorative acts.

Lewis Thomas wrote in *The Lives of a Cell*:

> We are beginning to treat the Earth as a sort of domesticated household pet, living in an environment invented by us, part kitchen garden, part park, part zoo. It is an idea we must rid ourselves of soon, for it is not so. It is the other way around. We are not separate beings. We are a living part of the Earth's life, owned and operated by the Earth, probably specialized for functions on its behalf that we have not yet glimpsed...We may be the greatest and brainiest of all biological opportunities on the planet, but we owe debts of long standing to the beings that came before us, and to those that now surround us and will help us along into the future.[2]

Psychology is the study or order (logos) of the psyche (soul). Contemporary practitioners, such as James Hillman and Sarah Conn, wonder why psychology in the past confined itself so narrowly to the personal self. It has not yet extended itself much to the individual in relation to social ills or other beings of the world, even though the pioneers of psychology, Freud (a biologist) and Jung (once an aspiring

---

2.   Lewis Thomas, *The Lives of a Cell* (New York: Penguin, 1978), p. 124.

archaeologist), believed that the deepest layers of the psyche were rooted in nature. As Jung wrote, "Our psyche is part of nature, and its enigma as limitless."[3]

Freud and Jung gave us a fundamental understanding of the workings of the "conscious" and "unconscious" parts of our selves. In this book "consciousness" includes our known skills, ideas, and use of language. The "unconscious" consists of all that is unknown, in addition to information from our personal past and world history, as well as potentials both for ourselves and the world. The everyday consciousness of an individual is referred to commonly as the "ego," which overlays the unconscious like topsoil over the lower layers. The ego is limited, the unconscious infinite. When awarenesses from the unconscious become known, they become part of the conscious mind. Unconscious knowledge comes to us largely through intuitions, dreams, and imaginative thought. "Conscious persons" try to know what is operating in and on themselves.

Everyone represses their greatest fears and desires into their personal unconscious. If we acknowledge them, the unconscious can become supportive and not threatening. A small or undeveloped ego that does not face up to this task remains cut off from the rich resources of the unconscious and causes the most harm in society. Before spiritual change can take place outwardly, our ideas and desires have to cross the threshold of consciousness.

Jung gave us the terms "collective unconscious" and "archetype" too. The "collective unconscious" phrase came about because people's dreams and imagery experiences contained details from past history that did not arise directly from their personal lives. "Archetype" referred to universal elements, such as "the tree of life," stars, circle, child, and notably the animals. They appear as common motifs in history, cultural myths, and dreams around the world. For the purposes of this book, I will concentrate on the animal archetypes, which are imprinted on the cells of our bodies and the recesses of our present and archaic memories. They are our heritage, but alive and dynamic in the present, available and calling to us.

---

3.   Carl Jung, *Man and His Symbols* (New York: Doubleday, 1972), p. 23.

In the realm of the "ecological unconscious," humans and nature are interconnected, all beings are related. Some of the fundamental ways, for instance, that humans are like other animals, include how much we share: the enjoyment of play, tendency to get scared, love our mates and offspring, demonstrate the capacity for altruism and compassion, revenge wrongs, feel shame, be mean and ornery, and prefer not to die. Like other animals, we communicate with gesture, stance, facial expression, and scent.

Animals are not just projections of ours. We must take care not to be anthropomorphic about them. They have their own unconscious, characteristics, inner states, and lifestyles. We must approach them in relationship that respects their integrity and needs. Even when animals appear in dreamtime, it's wise to see them as independent beings.

This shift in perspective—finding ourselves in the ecological unconscious rather than just the personal one—is aided by awareness of the merging of psychology of life with ecology, the science of systems in nature.

"Ecology" comes from the Greek, meaning study of homes. Our true home is Earth's biosphere. The principles of ecology are as grand as the symmetries of mathematics and physics. They include the major themes of predation and symbiosis, dry but useful terms to scientists for describing nature's systems. Predation gave rise to "survival of the fittest" ideas. Symbiosis—mutual dependency—is the current focus of attention. It includes parasites that feed on their hosts (not just like fleas but also the way people devour their nest). Mutualism refers to the way parts coexist or benefit one another. (Globalization is a social extension of that model.) Behind the jargon of ecology lies the music of the spheres, for ecology shows how nature is so skillfully organized, possessing of internal harmony or fitness, a mutual adaptation of parts, elegant in its entirety.

The boundaries in nature are quite elusive. Can we say our bodies stop at our skin, when they depend on food and water from outside, as well as disposal for our wastes? Change is also constant.

Degradation of habitats begins slowly, but then decline moves fast, inexorably. Signals appear in the diminished presence of migratory birds, the weakening chorus of frogs, the removal of keystone species upon which many others depend and the native flora and fauna. Ecosystems are resilient enough to withstand the elimination of one species, as another will take its place, but they begin to unravel and decay when too many are removed. While we might notice telltale signs in sparse vegetation, more difficult to spot are the subtle changes that take place in light, carbon dioxide, water, oxygen, temperature, acidity, salinity, presence of food, and diseases, all of which cause a chain of reactions. First to drop away are the species which require special conditions to survive. Then herbivores and their predators disappear. With the loss of other competitors, scavengers, and symbionts, populations crash. Deprived of genetic variability, populations cannot adapt and survive.

Because of the intricacy of the ecological web, the exact moment of ecosystem collapse is difficult to predict but experts agree that if enough species are extinguished in ecosystems throughout the world, the extinction of most other species will follow. By the time we find out if that is true, tragically it may be too late to do anything about it.

Why have animals become so threatened? The most severe problem is loss of terrain. Obviously populations of animals must nest, mate, and feed over a variety of suitable environments in order to thrive. Hemming them in onto limited refuges means an entire population could be destroyed by one fire or contagious disease. Road building, timber harvesting, and wetland draining have eliminated countless animal homes. Animals are also vulnerable to pollution of soil, water, and air caused by our industries and forms of transportation. They decline too because we over-collect them for zoos, museums, clothing, and exotic fetishes.

Population growth has radically altered ecosystems. From the time people domesticated animals our numbers have gone from six million to six billion.[4] According to the census counters of the United Nations, by the year 2015, the world population is expected to be between 7.1 and 7.9 billion by 2015, 21 billion by 2050. When biologists see this pattern of

---

4.   Niles Eldridge, *New York Times Magazine*, (December 5, 1999), p. 144. Eldridge is a curator at the American Museum of Natural History and author of *Life in the Balance: Humanity and the Biodiversity Crisis*.

population explosion of one species over others, they have learned that a species can destroy itself by fouling its own nest. Thus, our very proliferation may cause our extinction.

The Earth's systems have absorbed cataclysmic shocks and major extinctions of species in the past, but the current crisis is occurring at a much faster than previous ones—over a few decades rather than over thousands and/or millions of years.

In our busy lives we are so preoccupied with human affairs that we don't notice what is happening. At the same time we feel lonely and bemoan the lack of community. Could these feelings be related to our neglect of our ties to nature and that our real community includes all beings? This book will lead toward that possibility.

Meanwhile let's quickly review people's past attitudes toward animals to show how radical the changes have been.

For a long time, around 60,000–10,000 B.C., when people lived amidst animals more than they do now, animals were hunted, feared, and admired. People observed them closely and told stories about them. In caves around France and Spain they painted vibrant images of animals, full of movement and majesty, unparalleled since. In tribal cultures around the world masks of animals were made to absorb some of their power. The "animal people" were one society. If an animal was killed by a human, an offering was made to the gods or goddesses of creation for the taking. Our ancestors held animals in esteem and reverence. These details become part of our collective heritage.

Animals tutored early peoples. From animal sounds people contrived an alphabet. The hieroglyphs of the ancient Egyptians were based on animal images. Egyptians revered animals for their ability to fly, to smell keenly, to run swiftly or jump, to act instinctively, to communicate through body and eye contact as beyond their capacities and made many images of them in their sacred art. Animals were accepted in their duality—useful companions as well as dangerous, predatorial, and destructive. People were viewed as siblings of the animals, provided for by their solar god.

Shamans, who practiced healing from direct contact with the spirit world, often used animal sounds to induce the receptive state of consciousness, thus linking animal language with the gift of prophecy. The inner animals that guarded a person were considered as real as physical animals. In some cultures it was believed that when a child was born, an animal (or two or three) volunteered to be its protector. As the person grew, the animal would be replaced as needed. One of the major causes of illness was considered to be loss of the power animal.

American Indian cultures viewed nature as mother, father, friend, lover, and extended family. Animals were talked to and heard from. Energies were exchanged. Whether two-legged, four-legged, finned, or winged, all belonged to one spirit.

In the past, people tried to gain the friendship of an animal in order to be instructed by its sagacity. Nowadays such bonding is so rare that the relatively few modern people who make such a connection wax ecstatic. Loren Eiseley, the scientist-philosopher, considered a few sustained moments of play with a fox, tossing a bone back and forth, "the gravest, most meaningful act" of his life.[5] He wrote that "One does not meet oneself until one catches the reflection in an eye other than human.[6]

The factors contributing to the loss of respect for animals include the Judeo-Christian tradition that people had dominion over animals. In Genesis 1:28, it says:

> And God said unto them, Be fruitful, and multiply, and replenish the earth, and subdue it: and have dominion over the fish of the sea, and over the fowl of the air, and over every living thing that moveth upon the earth.

As humans increasingly focused on agriculture, animals became mere property. In art they were depicted as harnessed to human will; the human body was glorified. Rene Descartes, the 17th century philosopher, claimed that beasts could not think and therefore had nothing in common with rational man. People began to see themselves as both distinct from animals

---

5.   Loren Eiseley, *The Star Thrower* (New York: Harcourt Brace Jovanovich, 1978), p. 65.

6.   Loren Eiseley, *The Unexpected Universe* (New York: Harcourt, Brace & World, 1964), p. 24.

and superior to them. Our shared qualities with other species were pushed back into the unconscious. The thought that people can flourish apart from the rest of the living world is not uncommon. For this reason, the philosopher Gregory Bateson declared that this divided notion of self was the great epistemological error of western civilization.

Nowadays people hold a hodgepodge of views about animals. On the one hand, we raise our children with constant reference to animals. From farms, zoos, or books, children develop an awareness of them. We compare their hands to the paws of, say, raccoons, the way we walk upright to, say, monkeys or kangaroos, and the shape of our heads and torsos to others. Pictures show how ants form their communities or bees pollinate flowers. Pigs such as Wilbur and spiders like Charlotte, Winnie the Pooh bear and Eeyore the donkey are beloved. Those talking animals may be projections of their human authors but since we are all animals, we may understand intuitively from their body language what animals would declare if they could. (The mission of many wildlife magazines is to "speak for animals.")

Our language is filled with references to animals: we get "butterflies in the stomach" or a "frog in the throat." So-and-so "bugs" us or "gets my goat.")

But when people are detached and even alienated from animals, they also tend to be uncaring of themselves and are most likely to turn violent toward others. In this way, abusive behavior spreads like a contagion. We cannot be healed apart from this ailing relationship with animals.

Despite our attitudes, for eons animals have been knocking at the door of our minds. As Clarissa Pinkola Estes wrote, "No matter where we are, the shadow that trots behind us is definitely four-footed."[7] The images of animals in dreams, stories, art, and religions are of great interest because they have been formed spontaneously and are independent of the ego. This realm belongs to all but may be reflected on by individuals in their own way.

As self-regulating mechanisms of the psyche, dreams and contemplative imagery comment on a subjective situation by showing us what we are not

---

7.   Clarissa Pinkola Estes, *Women Who Run With the Wolves* (New York: Ballantine Books, 1992), p. xiii.

aware of. Usually such visions occur when our bodies come to rest—more precisely, when we stop using our egos to do tasks, and enter the realm of the unconscious (or reflection or prayer). The self that is synonymous with the center of our being is often symbolized by an animal that possesses the divine energy that exists within us and nature.

Dreams take us away from the surface of life to its deeper meaning. They correct our course in life, like a wind blowing our sails. They warn us about danger, predict some future events, and convey illuminating insights. Always the aim seems to be the wise, most optimum attitude toward life. Dreams cannot protect us from illnesses and sad events but do help in coping and understanding their significance in a larger framework. Dreams are often overlooked or belittled, but they are like getting FedEx packages from the soul's center. It's a shame to miss connecting with this supportive part of oneself.

In the "Myths and Dreams" section of each chapter of this book, I offer examples of specific animals and their meaning in people's lives. I have made no attempt to exhaust the evidence but instead seek to provide samples from a variety of cultural traditions, so that by the end the reader will be able to ramble along many paths. The question to keep in mind with images that resonate is: why are the animals appearing now and what do they have to say about healing one's life and the larger world? The problem pointed to is often familiar and relevant to all of us.

Inner relationship is about working with the thoughts and feelings aroused by our new awarenesses. Engaging in inner relationship with animals, they become powerful allies when we want to change our lives and restore our strength, dignity, and well being. We can become our own shamans.

The benefits are enormous and empowering. Letting animals into your heart sharpens senses, evokes visceral vitality, and awakens imaginations. The more we understand animals, the more we understand ourselves. Animal intelligence offers instruction in leadership and problem solving. Animals show us how to protect ourselves, how to be direct and upfront with anger, fear, tranquility. How to follow our hunger and real needs. They show us how to be courageous as well as how not to hold grudges.

They show us how to be alone. Identifying with them can center us in our solar plexus, make us tougher, less naive. Feeling kinship with them lessens our loneliness, because we have a sense of expanded community within and without.

Let us then re-vision our ties to animals by looking at the habits, the art, and the legends of animals. Let us look into our individual psyches and work with our hopes, fears, and sorrows, realizing that our pains are not separate from the world's. If we want to live in harmony with all, then we need to be aware of our thoughtforms about animals, for our destiny on Earth is more entwined than we may realize.

In this book then I invite contemplation of our "at-one-ment" with the grand continuum of life and to discover the meaning of that wisdom lying dormant within. "At-one-ment" implies atonement.

Obviously in this book I cannot cover every animal that exists. I have chosen those about whom we have the most charged feelings, such as bears, wolves, snakes, and deer. Since we are not as close to wild animals as domestic animals, we need to make more of an effort to include them in our comprehension of the world's community. Although many great animals do not appear in these pages, the format I offer can be applied to appreciating other animals' lives and their personal meaning.

Even though I must treat animals generically in these pages, remember, doing so is like generalizing about all the humans on the planet as if they are the same, when we know that every species is made up of individuals, who are very different from one another. Most of us tend to see dogs and cats as distinct personalities because we know them better. Wildlife biologists get more familiar with their subjects because of close observation. This familiarity helps. Just think what it would be like to describe ourselves as a species, using terms such as: 'they are omnivorous, mostly pair-bonding and copulating for pleasure, not just to produce offspring; they live singly or in groups; their young stay home for 17 years; parents share in feeding and housing them.' Yet, when we think of our features as a species, we can more easily appreciate similarities with and differences from other species.

In Part One and Two, each chapter showcases a particular animal—its characteristics, life from its point of view as much as possible, and its history with humans. Every chapter includes a section on examples from cultural mythology and the dreamscape, as stated before. In Part Three, chapter 13 explores practical restorative ways people are extending our boundaries beyond our human selves to include community with other animals. The last chapter presents detailed techniques for working with images so that the reader can know the excitement, fun, and enlightenment to be had by self-search. Thus, this book may be used as a reference and experiential guide.

I hope you will find much food for thought, guidance, and inspiration. As you read, notice what bright-eyed, feathered, furred, horned, beaked, and tailed animals pull on you, which ones make your skin tingle, what animals would you like to learn from?

PART ONE: Wild Animals

BEARS: GRAND MOTHER/FATHER

Relatively few among us have seen any bears, much less a grizzly, because they prefer to live unbothered and so have retreated to remote mountain ranges. Yet bears loom large in our ecological and imaginal landscapes. As an Indian chief said, "the great bear was made to be captain and rule the rest of the animals with wisdom and strength."

Pushed to the Edge

Its ancestors go back about 20 million years. At first the size of a small dog, bears grew larger and traveled to all the continents, modifying as they went and becoming what we call black bear, grizzly (brown), sloth bear, sun bear, spectacled bear.

White polar bears, the largest of all, developed about 125,000 years ago; in order to survive in the arctic their coats have hollow, reflective hairs that bounce sunlight down to their black skin, where heat is efficiently absorbed. Polar bears can swim up to 100 miles without rest, sprint 30 to 35 miles per hour and smell a seal through three feet of snow. Food shortages compelled them to dwell alone. Despite their solitary way of life in elements that seem fierce to us, they are extraordinarily playful and endearing in demeanor.

Capable of weighing about 1000 pounds, grizzlies stand flat-footed like us. When unthreatened, they move about calmly, poking into berry bushes, tussling with kin. While having a strong odor themselves, their noses can detect carrion nine miles away. If you come into their territory or carry a gun like the one that killed a relative or get too close to a mother's cubs, then they become ferocious and pop their jaw, yawn, lay back their ears, weave their head, and woof. One blow from a paw can knock off the head of a buffalo.

Bears can also be kind and gentle. A zookeeper tells the story of how a starved kitten entered the cage of a 500-pound grizzly bear during feeding time. Instead of attacking it, the bear pierced a bit of chicken meat with its claw and dropped it to the side of his dish. The cat quickly walked up and ate it. Soon the cat and the bear ate, slept and romped around the pen together.[8]

Bears may be more irritable if they are carrying around a chronic pain. They've been known to live with gunshot embedded in their lungs. They get abscessed teeth, probably due to their penchant for sweet foods. Losing their teeth in old age can result in starvation. They are also plagued by internal parasites and numerous injuries.

Yet they indulge in much play and wrestling, playing tag, tossing sticks, rolling around and grasping paws. To avoid nasty fights with each other, they observe a hierarchy in which large old males or females with cubs receive more deference than the other adults. They vocalize with an array of chomps, coughs, huffs, mumbles, howls, bellows, and bleats.

To satisfy their huge appetites, they need to forage over large territories. Unlike deer who graze, bears largely gather plants, enjoying berries, pine nuts, mushrooms, and leafy plants. Occasionally they feed on a mammal. To satisfy their desire for honey, they gulp quantities of bees, as if not caring about being stung. Bears eat ants, cutworm moths, and ladybugs. Two quarts of yellow jackets may go down.

Bears gorge on fish. They will stand along the edge of a stream and plunge after one when they see it. Or, they sit in the water and literally block the fish with their broad bodies. In former centuries, when salmon ran upstream to complete their life cycle, bears would wait for them. The first few they'd eat whole, then they would just eat the body and discard the head and tail. Finally they would select only females in order to eat the roe, leaving the carcasses for other animals. But since the logging of forests and dams in the lower 48 states have made rivers inhospitable to salmon, this support system has been destroyed.

---

8.   *Bozeman Daily Chronicle* (December 15, 1995).

Bears cram to eat before winter when food supplies diminish, and they will go dormant. For their hiding place, grizzlies often dig a den at the base of a tree or stump, with the roots serving as a protective ceiling. They make a floor out of layers of conifer branches. Black bears occasionally dig dens, but will often be satisfied with hollowed-out trees, natural caves, or dense thickets. Bears enter their dens when a winter storm comes along substantial enough to hide their tracks into the den.

Within a pregnant female's uterus is a free-floating embryo that began in early summer after mating but does not become implanted until after she settles down into the den. If resources are scarce, her body absorbs the embryos before they develop, thus leaving perhaps only two rather than four infants. For up to five months, she will not eat, drink, defecate, or urinate. She will lose fat but her lean body mass and bone actually increase.

(Scientists are trying to copy this process to help humans with osteoporosis. They also want to know more about how bear bodies do not build up urea, a toxic waste product of protein metabolism normally eliminated by kidneys, but instead recycle the urinary wastes to make protein. The energy for this process is contained in the bear's fat stores. If we could trigger the ability to go dormant, we might use it to help us endure a long challenge, such as a space flight.)[9]

The female bear gives birth to the cubs in the den after about eight weeks of gestation. In the ensuing solitude the cubs, weighing about a pound, blindly nestle against their mother's body, hear her heartbeat, and suckle. The cubs' long period of intimacy with their mother will help make them far more intelligent than most animals. When they emerge in the spring, they will stay very close to their mother for two or three years until she turns them away in order to conceive new young. In the meantime the sow guards her growing cubs closely.

Like us, bears dwell at the top of the food chain. Researchers estimate that a population of 2,000 grizzly bears requires about 50,000 square miles of relatively undisturbed habitat in order to have a 95% per cent chance of the population's survival for 100 years. Because grizzlies nowadays can't find that much contiguous land, their numbers have severely dwindled—

---

9.   New York Times (April 21, 1992), C1.

99% in the lower 48 states. Louisa Willcox, a longterm bear advocate, puts it, "It's as if they have been locked into the bathroom of the house and can't get from one room to another and are killed if they go out the door."[10] When bears are scattered in small groups or are separated from one another, they are much more vulnerable to genetic deterioration and disease and climate changes. Currently, grizzlies have decreased in number from about 100,000 to less than 1000.

While bears may have lost in the battle with us for territory, we are not the winners. Grizzlies are considered a "keystone" species, meaning that their presence indicates an ecosystem's health. Their failure to survive indicates that forests, rivers, and other animals are perishing too. Conversely, preserving adequate habitat for bear means clean and safe wilderness, from which all life benefits.

Bears are often killed legally and illegally for their body parts. A huge demand in Asia for the medicinal benefits of the bear's unique gallbladder (bear bile salts contain significant amounts of ursodeoxycholic acid) has led to the extermination of bears, even though the ingredients can be produced synthetically in labs and other alternatives used. Asians emphasize its importance in treating cancer of the liver, but it is also used in shampoos, lozenges, and teas. Bears are poached in the U.S. by trappers who can get around the lack of uniformity in state laws to supply the Chinese market. The meat of a whole bear may sell for $3000 in Japan. A soup of bear paws costs $400 in Thailand.[11]

Prior to the 19th century, bears coexisted with people but as our civilization "progressed," they were eliminated by gunfire and learned to fear humans. In the U.S., "mountain men," such as Davy Crockett, Jim Bridger, and Ben Lilly, were famous for going out with large numbers of dogs and killing 300–400 bears a year. Under such pressure, many bears no longer live more than five years, while an unmolested bear can live for 30 years or longer.

In the long term, bears do more for us alive than dead. It is a terrible irony that while countless fake "teddy bears," pictures of Smokey the Bear

---

10.   Presentation at Great Bear Conference (Bozeman, MT, May 24, 1996).

11.   Gary Brown, *Great Bear Almanac* (New York: Lyons & Burford, 1993), pp. 258-60.

and Winnie-the-Pooh pervade our society, the situation of real bears is so difficult.

Lost Teachings

"At first morning light, we hear bear mother's heart beat, the birth of her Sun is imminent," an old saying goes, reflecting how once upon a time bears were considered the first parents. The primary qualities of bears have traditionally held sacred meaning.

From earliest times people compared their lives to bears' and learned to survive from them. Recognizing shared tendencies for clowning, bluffing, stealing, and lazing around unless aggravated, they followed bears during migrations and learned where and how to find certain berries and medicinal plants. People learned to hoard food for winter. Bear caves made into temples have been found in the Alps dating from 50,000 B.C.E. In the Cult of the Master Bear native peoples did not call bears by their name but used some more deferential term, such as Grandfather or Grandmother, Honey Paws, Crooked Tail, or The Old Man with the Fur Garment. Native Indians believed that because animals were created before people, they were considered closer to the Great Spirit and thus more powerful.

The bear's withdrawal, fasting, and reemergence formed the basis for spiritual initiation rites of societies around the world. In some places people literally go into caves and fast in order to have a vision that will help them with a crisis in their lives. A model of resurrection, the bear not only awakens as if from the dead in spring but also with young. This event tells us that psychologically we too can return from the darkest hours with spirit reborn.

Hunting bears in some tribes was a sacred ritual. First a hunter tried to divine the outcome of a hunt through a dream. A positive dream boosted his confidence. Then he purified himself. Using a bow and arrow or gun was taboo, as these weapons were not equal to the bear's spirit. To capture the spirit of the bear was as important as its physical body. The Koyukons closed the bear's eyes after the kill to hide their stare. The dismemberment was done in a respectful sequence, the feet first. Every hair was considered to have a life of its own. A hide had power that could last for years.

Such native peoples respected the fact that animals had souls. In order to ward off retaliation, they would apologize for their killing, saying things like, "Do not be angry. I killed you only because I am poor and hungry. I need your skin for my coat and your meat so my family can eat."[12] Fortunately they were small enough in numbers so that bear populations were not adversely affected. The people believed the bear would be replenished too.

Talismans from a bear gave its possessor power, greatly needed to make it in the world. To get this power, you ate a piece of bear meat, danced a bear's life, and dressed yourself in fur and claws. These talismans helped people set aside their fears and replace them with the bear's courage and superior strength.

One fear was that of women. Part of our cultural inheritance includes a horribly long history of the fear of menstruating females. It was said that during women's periods, they "became bears." Some explanations have to do with the power of blood; others with the "teeth" in women's vaginas. An Indian story tells how a woman marries a bear, is attacked by her brothers, and ends up killing her mother and two of her brothers. In this story the woman turns bad because she married the bear; in other words, she became too wild and frightened the men. (Do we not see in our most repressive societies that women are subjected to the most controls?)

The association of bears with females is echoed as far back as the Greek reverence for a Bear Goddess and the way young girls danced in Her honor. Artemis was the Greek goddess of wild nature and the bear was one of her major incarnations or companions. It was Artemis who killed Callisto, one of her nymphs, for becoming impregnated by Zeus, and then feeling repentant placed her and her child among the stars as the constellations: Ursa Major and Ursa Minor. Artemis was also known as nurse and defendant of the newborn, like a mother bear.

---

12. David Rockwell, *Giving Voice to Bear* (Colorado: Roberts Rinehart Publishers, 1991), p. 60.

Later cultures amused themselves by capturing and making bears entertainers. During the years 470–1450 bears were led around on chains, performing little tricks on village streets. With their good coordination and amusing appearance, they could be taught to ride bicycles, toss balls, juggle, roller skate, skip rope, play the harmonica, eat with a knife and fork, and play dead. The circus was next. This image of bears is also part of our mythology.

Long ago the bear was addressed in a Finnish Rune as "my darling, honey-paws, my beauty,"[13] and today is likewise addressed by many scientists, photographers, and hikers who track living bears, using their own modern rituals of stalking, approach and capture with special equipment. Some spend long seasons in bear territory, hoping for acceptance by bears and jubilant about sightings. Then sacrificing their love for the wild, they traverse the nation's cities and plead with people to protect these dwindling species.

Grizzlies primarily stand for wilderness, where mettle and imagination are tested. Person after person has testified that being in their presence makes their hair stand on end ("I felt touched by an enormous power" is the refrain. Or "my life was changed."). Many think it is vital for our character that we feel some humility, knowing that in a face-to-face encounter we could be eaten, that we are not always in charge.

Wilderness awakens our minds, refreshes our bodies, frees our thoughts. Entering the wild, it takes some time to adjust and enter a more alert and receptive state of mind than usual. Forays into wild lands can be seen as a devotional practice, aimed at reconnecting to our true home, nature. While life in the wild is both violent and serene (likewise in cities), as author Pam Houston wrote: "In the wilderness, I feel not as though I am escaping the "real world" but that I am entering it. There is an essential part of myself that gets lost in my indoor life—a part as necessary and tangible as an arm or an eye—and I go to the wilderness to get it back."[14]

---

13. Ibid., p. 179.

14. Pam Houston, "The Bear in the Woods, the Bear in Us" (*New York Times,* Op-Ed, June 22, 1996).

Some people feel depressed, when they have to return to their towns or cities.

Bears are the supreme leaders of wilderness because they dominate the largest terrains and, significantly, provide safe haven for countless other animals. Thus, metaphorically, they are like the CEO's of huge corporations. Their leadership qualities are not lost on company executives, who invoke bears as mentors to improve company morale, help staff get over the fear of public speaking, work together cooperatively, or to solve hard problems not only with logic but with heart.

DREAMS & VISIONS OF BEARS

When bears appear in your thoughts and dreams, be aware of the bear's special qualities, life cycle, and political status. Reflect on the ceremonies and stories told about bears. The above material should give you enough leads to understand the messages of your specific images. Here are some examples of dreams from literature and individuals.

One of the bear's most poignant followers is Vietnam veteran, Doug Peacock. Traumatized by months of brutal slayings, he was too anxiety-ridden to settle into ordinary social routines and sought the solace of wilderness, as if in its rigor and solitude, he could find a match for his feelings. In one instance, he writes in *Grizzly Years*:

Half awake, I realized I had been dreaming. About war, I thought. The young grizzly's behavior reminded me of something. His reaction to the smell of danger—the presence of a larger boar or maybe the mating season in general—seemed to be to crawl back into the brush, hole up, and lie out this hazardous time. The same thing used to happen to me back in Southeast Asia; whenever the shit really hit the fan, when it looked as if we were about to be overrun and it became a matter of everyone for himself, my first impulse, or perhaps instinct, was to slide off alone into the jungle and keep going until I found vegetation thick enough to hide in, a sanctuary where I could ride out the hunt for Americans. So I thought I knew what it might feel like to be outgunned by bigger bears.[15]

He spent much of his recovery identifying with the bear in its facing of extreme circumstances. In another example, *The Ancient Child*, N. Scott Momaday portrays a character, who dreams of sleeping with a bear:

> The bear drew her into his massive arms and licked her body and her hair. It hunched over her, curving its spine like a cat, until its huge body seemed to have absorbed her own. Its breath which bore a deep, guttural rhythm like language, touched her skin with low, persistent heat.[16]

This bear restores the woman to her connection to animals and nature. Nomaday says that he likes to identify with bears: "I have this bear power. I turn into a bear every so often. I feel myself becoming a bear."[17] Others have notably similar visions.

Many of us say we need to "hibernate" or "den" to regenerate or create. We feel the need to withdraw from our public obligations to a solitude wherein we can write or compose a work that requires uninterrupted concentration to think through and bring into being. A woman who withdrew to a remote cabin in winter said that after she started a journal, she dreamed <u>I followed bear tracks to a den. She came out, dazed. I was afraid it would kill me.</u> Far from it. She found that she started writing more deeply than ever.

A common motif is of dream with <u>a bear in the basement.</u> A powerful ally is near, and the dreamer would do well to bring the bear "upstairs."

Bears "bear" us often in dream journeys. They carry us and help us give birth, just as the etymology of their name suggests. Once I dreamed that <u>I was being carried on the back of a she-bear. I felt myself moving with the</u>

---

15.   Doug Peacock, *Grizzly Years* (New York: Henry Holt, 1990), p. 142-3.

16.   N. Scott Momaday, *The Ancient Child* (New York: Doubleday, 1989), p. 29.

17.   Charles Woodard, *Ancestral Voices: Conversations with N. Scott Momaday* (Lincoln, NE: University of Nebraska Press, 1989).

powerful muscles in her shoulders. Later she/we gave birth to a cub. At the time I was carrying a gigantic task alone. Capturing some of the muscular force of the bear gave me the strength I needed to meet the challenges involved in the work. The image of giving birth to a bear cub augers greatness in the sense of significance, not necessarily fame.

Another woman, when she was pregnant, often sang to a she-bear to give her strength. Although married, she began wanting to leave her husband and identify herself as a lesbian, but she feared that her husband would take her child away from her. She lived in a conservative community where the court probably would have been unsympathetic. She wore bear jewelry, placed claws and bear figurines around her home. She felt in retrospect that her bear healed her wounds and gave her the courage "to be me and go for my joy, love my baby, and not let anyone mess with me." One of her dreams was:

I was floating in a river. Downstream a big bear with a cub was catching fish. I tried to be quiet but suddenly the big mama galloped toward me and bellyflopped right in my face. She asked, what did I feel? Fear was my answer. The bear said that she was not going to kill me, that I should feel happy. I felt extremely powerful.

She said the bear has also helped her accept feeling fat by showing her that it is okay to be large and take up a lot of space, be brawny and intimidate people, to enjoy lying around and eating.

Because polar bears have a different ecology from grizzlies, those distinctions must be taken into account when they appear in dreams. A man dreamed of a polar bear at a time when he loved a woman with whom he worked, but while she did not return his love, they still had a long project to complete. Everyday he would go to work and come home, feeling as if his body was sliced and bleeding. Although she was pleasant enough to him, his unfulfilled desire made him feel frustrated and desolate. When he had the dream, he realized that in this situation he was living in a cold region. While the atmosphere was frosty, the polar bear was able to not only survive in it but to play in it with warmth and energy. He found a picture of a polar bear who wore an extremely beneficent expression. The polar bear sustained him through this period.

Bear images give us the strength and awareness to be fierce when we need to protect our territory and generous and playful as well. They are guardian spirits who show us how to satisfy big hungers and stand tall and broad. These mentors know how to survive in the most rugged territory; they perish in over-development.

In 2004 a four year study of the warming of the Arctic Circle was released by a committee of eight nations that described the retreats of glaciers and sea ice, thawing of permafrost and shifts in the weather and global atmosphere. The report stated that polar bears, ice-living seals and the local people dependent on them for food are experiencing dire consequences.

We must remember that, as James Hillman has written:

> Beyond all interiorizing of the bear—bringing it "inside" and taking its image as representing a potential within our own personal selves—is the bear itself. Beyond "instinct," beyond "theophany" is the utterly free-moving spirit of the great white bear in each of these dreams, calling, even piteously, to be seen, to be heard. Like Behemoth, that animal tremendum who brings all discussion to a conclusion at the end of the Book of Job, the great white bear baffles human comprehension. Yet, like Behemoth, whom, the Bible says (Job 40:15), God made at the same moment as he made humans, the animal tremendum may therefore be a coequal, coeternal brother.[18]

To lose the presence of bears in our lives—inner and outer—would be to lose a marvelous greatness of spirit.

---

18. James Hillman, *Dream Animals* (San Francisco: Chronicle Books, 1997), p. 45.

WOLVES: Extra-sensory Strategist

Snapshots from a life

Scene: A wolf howling. The canyons and cliffs are obscured in the dark night. A lone wolf sets its head skyward and sends forth tremulous chords from deep in its throat. Soon that cry in the dark is answered by one, then several others. Several wolves will find each other again, eager to join in the singing, harmonizing on different notes rather than chorusing on the same one. The howling may reveal where a pack has found a coyote, or, advise newcomers where they should not trespass.

Wolves are heard in the few wild places where they can survive. Larger than coyotes, with muscled chests, long lean legs, and big paws, wolves circle around vast ranges, not migrating, but going in search of food and dens and rendezvous sites. As they trot around, they help the ecosystem: their fur disperses seeds, their kills are fed upon by birds, foxes, and other animals; carcasses decompose and add humus to the soil, supporting more lush growth that attracts small animals, which in turn attract predators of their own; abandoned dens are taken over as homes by small mammals, such as porcupines.

These bouncy carnivores evolved from canids that emerged about three million years ago, producing jackals in the eastern hemisphere and coyotes in the western. The first wolves are thought to have split from the coyote line about one million years ago, with the gray wolf emerging about 700,000 years ago and eventually loping all over Eurasia and North America. The color of their thick fur blends with the colors of prairie, forest, tundra or desert they inhabit.

Wolf brains are large in the areas that handle sense impressions; they process information swiftly. A domestic dog's brain is about 30% smaller in comparison. Compared to humans, they smell 100 times more acutely and hear 16 times more. Although near-sighted, they can see much more than humans in the dark. They can read each other's scat and urine to tell the depositor's sex, age, physical and emotional state. They understand subtleties in the textures of rocks and dirt. Their personalities can be gentle, mischievous, clownish, shy or outgoing. They have dark markings on their muzzles, ears, eyes, and tail tips that help express anger, fear, resignation, joy, and sorrow.

In the wild wolves live about five years. Practicing their own population control, they will kill each other if their habitat gets stressed.

Scene: A pup sits at his father's feet and looks up at him eagerly. The father's bushy tail is up, his mouth open ready to regurgitate food. A wolf's family consists of a mother, father, the young, and several relatives, with every member filling a role that may change according to the needs of the pack.

In wolf society only the highest-ranking pair mates. The subordinate females will not become fertile, which keeps the birthrate down to one litter per pack per season, but the other wolves are still important in helping raise the young. During estrus, which lasts 5 to 15 days between January and April, a female's urine, menstrual blood, and secretions emit odors that greatly arouse the male. He will lick a spot on which the female has urinated and then urinate on it himself as part of the process of forming a bond with her and synchronizing their reproductive cycles. They frolic for weeks, with the female soliciting and rejecting the male's advances, or placing her head and paws on the male's neck, or both grabbing each other's snouts.

The pair have an extraordinary copulation. At the height of her heat, the female allows the male to mount her. A bulb at the base of his penis enlarges in order to lock behind the female's strong vaginal muscles. They stay locked together for as long as 30 minutes, even if the male dismounts and twists to the side, an interval during which he can safely ejaculate his sperm several times.

Male and female wolves often stay together, unless separated by perils of death, man, or pestilence. The female decides where they will settle to den and hunt for about six weeks. She gives birth in early May to an average of six pups, although the number fluctuates according to environmental challenges. The father and other unmated wolves bring the mother and pups chunks of food. For the puppies they regurgitate the contents of their stomachs and pass food from mouth to mouth. The puppies lick the face of any adult who comes to the den to see what they have for them.

After about 10 weeks, wolves leave their dens and move the pups to the first of a series of playgrounds. Four of the six pups are likely to die from early stresses. The remaining young wolves stay with the adults through the first winter, learning how to be part of a team, how to hunt—backtrack, circle and come up behind an enemy. By the following spring some wolves will stay on with the pack as adults, but others will leave. They take care not to overlap hunting and breeding territories by scenting trees and stones just as we do with red paint and fences.

Scene: Wolf pack circling moose. Wolves may be quick and agile in a chase, but they know they can't kill a big animal on their own. One quarter the size of a grizzly, wolves can be killed by the strong slashing hooves of a moose, elk, or deer if they get too close. A broken jaw would mean starvation. Wolves thus strategize and cooperate as teams in order to be successful, especially in winter when it's tough to get a good meal.

When a wolf first gets wind of prey a mile away, it cocks its ears and joins with the others. The wolves wag tails, stretch, make noises, building excitement just like athletes before a big game. A male or female leads the pack single file toward a herd of moose or elk or deer. The pack disperses and tests the prey to determine vulnerabilities and single out a weak, sick, injured, or old animal. Working together and in shifts, they attempt to distract the animal by seizing its muzzle in front or dragging on its flank, until finally the animal collapses.

Wolves do not capture most of the animals they go after; only about 4% of their forays end in a feast. In a wild ecosystem, wolves will try to drive out coyotes, their competitors and keep moose, deer, and elk populations from exploding and overgrazing the area. To prevent eagles, wolverines, and foxes, among others, from taking their food, wolves will either kill these animals or cache their meat. But they do not kill ravens because it appears that ravens lead them to places where they may find prey.

Scene: Wolf lying on ground, body rigid from the internal havoc wreaked by poison. Wolves of all species suffered almost complete extermination by humans in this country and Eurasia. Before the arrival of Europeans in this country, wolves thrived in every region. In the early 1600's the colonists brought and raised livestock. Presidents George Washington and Thomas Jefferson promoted a wool industry. If one or two wolves killed sheep, all wolves were blamed, even though feral dogs were known to have killed many more sheep.

In the 1840's–60's when the gold rush lured people westward, men were paid $2 a hide to clear wolves out. The big herds of buffalo upon which the wolves subsisted disappeared. The lands where they roamed freely were fenced off and populated with livestock. Soon starving, some wolves preyed upon the domestic animals. In retaliation death traps were set out, and settlers made a profession out of killing wolves that went far beyond predator control.

Between 1859 and 1940 the wolf was extirpated here without remorse…

Wolves died in pits with the bottoms made wider than the tops so they couldn't climb out. The pits were baited with meat and covered with branches. Sometimes sharpened stakes were set at the bottom to pierce them as they fell in. Wolves were caught and killed in their unlockable sexual embrace. Their heads and feet were lassoed and pulled apart. They were clubbed to death, shot at with automatic weapons from airplanes. In the spring their dens were raided and their pups murdered. Trappers made snares of wire nooses that killed millions of other animals too. (In Alaska it was found once that within a two month period 134 wolves were trapped, 37 were still alive (some had chewed off a leg to get free), but also trapped were 35 moose, 14 caribou, 4 golden eagles, 26 red foxes, and other small animals.) The killers made steel traps that clamped through to the bone but most of all they laced buffalo and other prey with strychnine.

A diary recorded that one night one poisoned buffalo carcass on the Kansas plains caused the deaths of "thirteen big gray wolves, fifteen coyotes and about forty skunks." By 1945 only a few wolves were left here and there.[19]

No other animal has been so attacked with such prejudice and hatred as wolves. No amount of killing seemed to assuage man's need to do it. But the tide turned when people started realizing that many animals were being driven to extinction.

The Endangered Species Act in 1973 declared wolves endangered in every state except Alaska and Minnesota where it is listed as threatened, which meant that federal agencies were required to bring back "viable populations." It took about two more decades for reintroduction programs to be authorized.

Recovery plans called for the continuance of 10 breeding pairs (10 packs or 60–100 wolves) over three years, a number biologists determined was necessary to maintain genetic diversity and sustain minimal numbers of animals through disease and adversity. After reaching that level, the wolf can be delisted, which means hunting seasons could be opened on them. The programs, which are taking place in Yellowstone National Park, in selected sites in northwest Montana, central Idaho, the Southwest, Tennessee, N. Carolina, and the northeast, have reported sure signs of success. Although recovery, which requires state funding from hunting and fishing license sales and tax on firearms, has cost no more than the salary of one football player, it faces constant political challenges. These "recovered" wolves will never be free from human observation and intervention.

The future of wolves and ecosystems is tenuous. Much depends on the human psyche and how we respond to wolves.

Obsession

Whenever humans blame or praise others obsessively, it is a psychological assumption that some part of the person's self is being

---

19.   Barry Lopez, *Of Wolves and Men* (New York: Scribners, 1978), p. 191-3.

unconsciously projected onto another. Given this hypothesis we need to take responsibility for our projections onto wolves, especially when we destroy them without a factual basis. We don't have to love wolves, but we should not use them as scapegoats.

Over the span of time people felt fear, hatred, admiration, curiosity, and delight for wolves. We've inherited a mixture of beliefs. Long ago the "good mothering" aspect of wolves was respected and even desired. The twin founders of the city of Rome, Romulus and Remus, were depicted in a sculpture showing them being suckled by a wolf. This image suggested that the great city sprang from humans with a deep attachment to wolfdom. Tu Kueh, the legendary founder of the Turkish nation, as well as the heroes, Zoroaster and Siegfried, were also reputed to have been suckled by female wolves. Many Indo-European pagan peoples claimed that they were descended from wolves and held names with "wolf" or "wulf," as in the Anglo-Saxon epic *Beowulf*. The idea of werewolves actually originated in people's seeing their gods, and especially goddesses, in their wolf aspect. But this bond with wolves went underground for a long spell as the Christian Church turned the ancient wolf cults into demonic legends and persecuted people for their beliefs.

Among Judeo-Christian peoples if a wolf killed a person or any "property" (a term that includes domestic animals), the individual felt morally bound to kill the wolf. Predators in the wild came to be regarded as threats to a subdued, pastoral countryside; thus it was acceptable to get rid of them. (Note how it is called "sport" when a man kills an animal, yet "malicious" if an animal attacks him.) King Edward of England in the 10th century allowed people to pay their taxes with wolves' heads and their fines with wolves' tongues. In England the last wolf was killed in 1500, in Ireland 1770, in Denmark 1772. By the 19th century wolves were rare in France and Germany, with but a lone survivor or two in the 20th century. Throughout this time animals were said to have no souls, so no man need feel guilty for doing away with them.

These Europeans, just as those who settled our country, were afraid of wolves and the dangers lurking in the wild as they walked or rode about the countryside. They originated the stories, "Little Red Riding Hood," in which the enemy is a cunning, devouring wolf, and "Three Little Pigs," which advises making a house strong enough to ward off the wolf. Anything that threatened existence, such as famine or a sexual aggressor, was labeled a "wolf". The "hour of the wolf" was known as the middle of the night when the devil appeared. These people painted their fears onto wolves without understanding that wolves were a mirror of their thoughts.

Our ancestors who came to this country brought with them their heritage of beliefs and wolf bounties. Here in 1756 John Adams said, "The whole continent was one continued dismal wilderness, the haunt of wolves." The pioneers had a tough time, hacking homes and food out of this wilderness. Even though to our eyes they were lucky enough to witness some of the most awesomely beautiful landscapes of America, the prevailing attitude was that nature was hostile and there for exploitation.

Those who worked the land and raised cattle and sheep saw the wolf as a competitor and an outlaw. They were bothered that wolves lived free on land that they had to pay for and to struggle on. Furthermore, wolves were wily and could outwit them. The fact was that ranchers and farmers lost more animals through disease and drought (e.g. the Depression years) or severe winters than they ever did to wolves. They couldn't do anything about these disasters, but they could do something about the wolf. The wolves thus became the target for all their resentment over losses.

These people called the wolf greedy, rapacious, deceptive. But those qualities characterized those people who picked off the gold, land, Indians, and buffalo at will. Many of these people were greedy for profits, devious in their approach, and often lawless. The historian Patricia Limerick, author of *Trails: Toward a New Western History*, said, "Nature, having had the effrontery to frighten and intimidate Euro-Americans in their first meetings, was going to pay for that very costly, and very temporary, initial victory."[20]

As history shows, a dangerous obsession of mind took over. The killing of wolves went way beyond predator control. Wolves were tortured gloatingly. People poisoned their own family members in their frenzy to

---

20.   Patricia Limerick, Presentation at the Greater Yellowstone Coalition Conference, (Bozeman, MT, May 31, 1996).

attack wolves. As far back as 1927, the U.S. Biological Survey and other groups investigated the hundreds of stories about murderous wolf packs in newspapers and books and found that they were false, that no court of law would recognize any fact upon which they were based. Wolf authority David Mech has said there is no record of a wild healthy, non-habituated, wolf seriously injuring a human anywhere in N. America. By comparison, more than 20 people are killed and three million attacked each year by the domestic dog.[21]

In historian Limerick's analysis, after the settlers had irreversibly established their power and dominance, then they felt safe enough to admit that wildlife could be guided, led, even learned from, as long as it was done on human terms. People were also finally revolted by the cruelty of the trapping devices and raised their voices against them and their users.

The wolf reintroduction plans addressed human concerns in order to facilitate success. For instance, to reduce conflicts between ranchers and wolves, biologists who work for the US Fish and Wildlife Service must notify ranchers about any sightings of wolves in the neighborhood. The ranchers are not allowed to shoot wolves (though they do because it's easier than dealing with officials). The wolves are darted with tranquilizers and monitored by radio-activity and removed if they kill a domestic animal. Defenders of Wildlife volunteered to compensate ranchers for livestock or sheep losses.

Now polls show that most people favor reintroduction. Why did the national psyche change? As wilderness vanishes before our eyes, and urbanized people realized their remoteness from the natural world (so different from the colonists who felt overwhelmed by it), bringing wolves back symbolizes the possibility of recovering the precious wildness we lost in the all-consuming obliteration of it. The reintroduction of wolves has been accompanied by intense enthusiasm and sentiment.

And some of these supporters include ranchers and former trappers. Toxie E. Beavers, a Texas cattle rancher and former hunting guide, said that after he read what he could, he "climbed over side of the fence to help

---

21.   Defenders of Wildlife Fact Sheet; Biologue Series, Prepared by the U.S. Fish and Wildlife Service, Dept. of the Interior, 1994.

the wolf in general and the Mexican wolf in particular." Leo Cottenoir, the man who shot the presumably last wolf in Yellowstone Park in 1943, is full of regret. Now he says, "I think God made the wolf and he's got just as much right to be here as any other God-given animal....Man is the biggest damn predator around." Hoping to spot another wolf before he dies, he has joined the hordes of wolf-spectators at Yellowstone.[22]

Allowing wolves to roam in some ecosystems brings up certain moral questions. One is whether or not humans have the right to decide whether wolf species will live or die? We have seized that right, yet some regard our doing so as a violation of nature's law that all organisms are equally important in the fabric of being. Another is whether or not wolves and other animals have feelings and rights to their way of life, space, and freedom? These questions will be taken up in Part Three of this book.

Suffice it to say that biologists have shown us how although wolves are superior in extrasensory perception, they share with us many qualities. Humans and wolves are sociable, enjoying warm, companionable, emotional lives. We are individualistic. We play roles within the family, community, and organization. We have hierarchies of authority and standing, positions for which they compete. We evolved as group hunters and are predators. We use strategy and coordination to create a social system that protects and enables the group to achieve its goals. We care deeply for our young. We enjoy companionship, song, smiles, recreation, and affection, yet can be aggressive and violent. We can be altruistic and cooperative, as well as ruthless and domineering. Ideally, the way to integrate wolves is to open up land so they can thrive and to open our psyches to their presence in dreams and visions.

DREAMS & VISIONS OF WOLVES

As just described, the inner beliefs people have held regarding wolves have severely affected their survival on this earth. Regardless of our attitudes, the wolves have done the best they could to thrive. Contrary to the false negative beliefs, in some cultures wolves have been sacred.

---

22. Brandon Loomis, *High Country News* (February 6, 1995), p. 13.

Indians, for instance, viewed wolves as an embodiment of the Great Spirit. Just as Indians learned from wolves, so too may we allow wolves to help shape our character. However, as we make room for wolves in an effort to share physical and psychic space with them, we must equalize the balance of power. In making the effort, it would help us to remember that our souls—the fire and moral center of our being—are linked to their survival, that when we kill them, we kill a piece of ourselves.

When you dream about wolves, single out which qualities of the wolf—such as liveliness, fight, hunger, sagacity, or perceptiveness—are being emphasized. Consider how you can increase any of these in your life. Even if the wolf acts as if he or she is chasing you in order to eat you, and in the dream you are terrified, it is most likely that the wolf wants your attention. If you spend some time reflecting on that wolf pursuing you, then later a dream will come in which you and the wolf are in a friendlier relation. In your life too you will find yourself behaving with more energy, particularly with the quality that is being emphasized about the wolf.

Here are two dreams that came to a woman in one night, showing the progression from terror to peaceful love. This pretty woman was anxious about most areas of her life. She had been abused as a child, run over by a car, become an alcoholic who had tried suicide. As the years went by in sobriety, her life improved, and she found good jobs and relationships. She was extremely shy about her gifts as an artist and poet, although intense about the rights of people treated poorly. She described this dream as "the most extraordinary of my life."

Was with a dear friend, Ginny. Others turn against her. Ginny becomes a wolf and bites a little rabbit in half. The dreamer feels horrified. The she-wolf seemingly wants to kill me. I am in grave danger. A dark shaman, the only one who can kill this wolf and thus save my life, goes up the mountain and into a snowstorm to track and kill the wolf. He is killed. I am hiding in terror on a bathroom floor. The she-wolf tears through the building to get to me, chews her way through the floor, and is upon me. But

instead of killing me, she lays down on me and embraces me with her paws. She is wounded, huge, bluish gray. She may not live. I think: I love you! I love you. I AM you!
(I awoke with feelings of overwhelming, heartbreaking love for the wolf who is me. Then later I dream:)
I ascend with the wolf into the night sky, full of stars. We are going to become a constellation together. We will be eternal. I am holding the wolf, she is holding me. We are peaceful.

In this dream sequence she starts off loving a female side of herself. When feeling attacked, she experiences shame, a buried feeling that persisted more than she was aware. This unacknowledged aspect turns into a powerful wolf. At first the wolf appears threatening, even outwits a strong masculine figure, but the wolf turns out to be a wounded part of herself. It is wonderful that she can feel love for this nurturing animal. Her embrace of the she-wolf, the image of their forming an eternal constellation, are like talismans that she will be able to touch for their enduring strength in the future. As long as she remembers the wolf-part of herself, she will be much more secure and competent in her life.

A woman described going on a shamanic journey, when she was seriously ill, and having a profound experience in which a she-wolf invited me to nurse alongside her pups. When I accepted her invitation, my body was flooded with feelings of bliss. I felt completely accepted, totally comfortable, and at home. This dream harkens back to the ancient, enduring and thus archetypal nurturing wolf.[23]

Many of us find in the soulful howling of a wolf the sounds of our own yearning for wildness and pain, ranging from sorrow to loneliness and deprivation. Like the wolf, we too want to howl with longing from the melancholy of isolation. We also, like wolves, want to howl with joy when we experience satisfying communion with others, deeply releasing sexual unions, and heroic triumph.

---

23. Anne Firestone, "Wolf in the Human Psyche" (*Spirit of Change Magazine*, Fall 1994), p. 35.

The books of Jack London, *Call of the Wild*, and Clarissa Pinkola Estes, *Women Who Run With the Wolves,* attest to this longing for wildness and freedom of thought and being. Author Rick Bass frequently warns that if we push wolves into a dead-end place of no-mystery, no-wildness, we will follow. Fortunate is the person who stays connected, avoiding the soul-death of the spirit. A child who later became a patient of Sigmund Freud's had a dream, which he experienced as terrifying but would remain numinous for his lifetime.

> I am lying in bed at night, looking out over the foot of my bed through casement windows at a row of walnut trees. It is winter and the old trees are without leaves, stark against the snow. Suddenly the windows fly open and there sitting in a tree are six or seven wolves. They are white, with bushy tails, their ears cocked forward as though they were listening for something. I awake screaming.[24]

This portentous dream offers a vision of immense significance, given that the wolves are white and there are so many of them. Holding such wolves in the house of your psyche without turning your back in fear could keep you open to the elements of nature, heighten your sensory awareness, and lead to harmony rather than alienation from wild animals. Through inner dialogue with the wolves during the course of your life, you could bring their knowledge about strategy, play, bonding, or fight to bear on your problems.

Wolves can teach us how to face the dangers of life and keep moving even while injured. Their strong resolve can help us attack our culture's wrongs and cruelties. Their presence in our consciousness can aid us in eluding nay-sayers or those who throw water on our creative fires. They encourage us to explore, loop back and circle around, defend ourselves with ferocity.

The warrior aspect of wolves was honored by the Egyptians, who made the wolf-headed god Upuaut leader of the army. Ally of Osiris, Upuaut

---

24.   Barry Lopez, *Of Wolves and Men* (New York: Scribners, 1978), p. 267.

meant "he who opens the way" and his image emblazoned shields. Anubis was one of his chief officers in conquering the world. Among the Norse cultures, in Valhalla Odin sat with two wolves at his feet and ruled his empire.

The ability to strategize and lead offensives when necessary is one of the wolf's talents. Yet, wolves have such mastery that when they return home, tired and worn, from an all night's hunt for food, they become completely gentle as the pups greet them, hit on their bodies, and frolic.

Thus, wolves move in and out of our psyches. They may now be confined to a tiny percentage of bounded wildlands, and although many of us never see real ones, they still appear in dreams, making all that they embody known to us.

SNAKES: BRAID OF SKILLS

Like a waking dream: I am walking with a friend one day in a refuge in southern Pennsylvania. We start to cross a bridge over a river, when I look down and see a snake in the muddy flats. In its mouth it grips a wide catfish and drags it, undulating backward onto dry land. I can't resist watching. My friend, however, takes one horrified glance, and hurries over the bridge. Once the catfish stops moving, the black snake positions itself to expand its jaws around the catfish's head, which seem at least three times broader than the snake's. Slowly, fraction by fraction, the snake encompasses the catfish's head until the whole catfish is engorged and gone from view.

One of the things snakes do is eat injured and sick fish, thereby strengthening the fish population in a river. And it eats its meal whole, using jaws that are not hinged as ours are. An anaconda can even encompass a deer. A meal will be slowly digested and will last the snake several weeks.

This approach to eating is just one way snakes seem strange to us and therefore frightening. Some scientists say that the abhorrence of snakes has been around so long that it is stamped on our genes. But the fear of snakes has also resulted in peoples' putting snakes on a pedestal and revering their special characteristics. We create narratives about snakes but for clarity we should try to understand their lives, separate from our reactions to them.

One Who Can Live Anywhere

Snakes evolved over 100 million years ago, as nature seemed to experiment with a lizard sans arms and legs. (The boa constrictor still has spurs that are leg vestiges.) Their tubular bodies contain major organs that are staggered linearly. Their esophagus extends to their stomach in the middle of their body. From lizard days snakes grew in length; they range from the five-inch blind snake to the 30-foot anaconda or reticulated python. They swelled too. The 30-foot anaconda can weigh 600 pounds. Snakes move their elongated torsos by contracting their muscles with dazzlingly complex and swift ease. Their watertight scales enable them to live virtually anywhere—underground, in forests, deserts, and the sea. Their scales grow like our fingernails, can be sloughed off, and remade. Their features make them one of evolution's supreme accomplishments of adaptability.

Their bodies look like wild braids, decorated with stripes, lozenges, diamonds in vivid reds, yellows, and blues. The endangered San Francisco garter snake has red on its head, along with a greenish-yellow stripe edged with black, a broad red stripe edged with black on its side, and a turquoise blue belly. Since recorded history, people have patterned cloth after the colorful, geometric designs on snakeskins.

Some species have long and pointed heads, others chunky. Because snakes have no eyelids, their eyes always seem open, which has given them a reputation for being "all-seeing." Their phenomenal hinged jaws and elastic skin enable them to encompass an enormous range of prey: earthworms, slugs, snails, crabs, spiders (even tarantulas), scorpions, beetles, frogs, lizards, egrets, and bats. Some can lash their bodies around a creature like a rope and squeeze, so that their victim cannot inhale and eventually dies from lack of breath. All this costs them much energy, so they seek nutritious meals that will last a long time.

Perhaps because snakes dwelled underground once, where eardrums are easily damaged, they have no eardrum like other burrowing animals and are "stone deaf." Thus, they rely on other means to orient themselves. They can sense vibrations through the ground; for instance, they respond to impending earthquakes long before we are aware of them. The "pit" vipers have a unique spot between the nostril and eye, which detects infrared radiation (i.e. heat) precisely, enabling them to determine the presence of other creatures in complete darkness. Snakes' soft and harmless tongues help taste and smell things, flick when suspicious.

Snakes fill niches in ecosystems as both predator and prey. As predators, venomous snakes are the most famous but are actually least numerous or dangerous. Snakes are prey for hawks, owls, possums, pigs, skunks, and cats, although their biggest enemies are humans who kill them with knives, pistols, and cars. While not very swift and with relatively fragile teeth, to defend themselves they will try to avoid detection, flee when discovered, and if cornered feign threats before actual combat. A hognose snake will puff up like a venomous cobra, even though it lacks venom, just to scare. If that does not deter the enemy, the snake can imitate death throes by writhing, hissing, rolling over, defecating, and finally becoming still as if it had stopped breathing. Then when the enemy turns away, the snake will quickly slither away into hiding.

Snakes use their sinuous bodies and chemosensory skills in sexual play. A male may undulate his body in waves, flick his tongue on the female's back, and bite her. Competing males rear up and entwine their necks, attempting to force each other to the ground. A single female, exuding attractive pheromones, can be entwined in a ball with a dozen males. Sometimes a female will mimic another male in battle, testing the courage of the other males. They roll around and explore one another for hours at a time. When the female decides she has a winner, she opens her cloaca and allows the male to emit inside her. Does nature have a grand old time or not?

The female will look for a private humid place to fertilize her eggs. She can hold off seven years under deprived circumstances.

We need more than ever to be aware of snakes' continued existence in the world or else they may be heard about just in stories or on television. Snakes today, along with other reptiles and amphibians around the world, are declining more rapidly than other species. About 200 species of snakes are now listed as threatened or endangered. Loss of habitat is the main reason—our cutting down of forests, especially in tropical areas such as Ecuador, and elimination of prairies. Toxic poisoning from agricultural pesticides also takes a huge toll. The conservation of snakes unfortunately does not get as much attention as other animals, perhaps because of latent human repugnance. A sad state of affairs, given that biologists believe many snakes have yet to even be named.

Held In Contempt and Awe

The following story of Kuki Gallmann exemplifies an individual's extraordinary capacity to love and live with snakes despite good reason for hatred. This account appears in her book (adapted into a movie), *I Dreamed of Africa*.

Kuki is an Italian woman who married a man, for whom she uprooted herself and moved to Africa. He died not long afterward in an accident. When her son reached adolescence, he became fascinated by the many snakes that lived around them in Kenya. He began catching harmless ones, keeping them in cages in the stables. He photographed them and wrote down his observations about their size and growth in extensive "Snake Diaries." Kuki never liked snakes, was not enthusiastic about his hobby, but felt she should not stifle his serious interests.

In her book she wrote, "Sooner or later some of the snakes caught were poisonous ones, as I had always feared, and which I had originally forbidden."[25] As a precaution, she brought in an expert to work with her son. Nevertheless, her son was bitten—again and again—and yet was still intent on collecting snakes. He made a huge pit for about a hundred various snakes. He planted bushes to attract insects. Birds came for the insects, and the snakes snapped for the birds.

The teenager wrote in his diary: (Puff adders are) "responsible for more human deaths than any other African snake…(Their) poison destroys blood cells in body and attacks tissues."[26] Although he had been bitten by them and knew that a body can only incorporate so much poison, he, nevertheless, continued to milk them for their venom. He would push a glass jar against the fangs of the snake and squeeze its gland. The venom could then be crystallized and used to make anti-toxin serum. It takes 69,000 extractions to make one pint of their poison. Such venom is used

---

25.   Kuki Gallmann, *I Dreamed of Africa* (New York: Penguin, 1991), p. 157.
26.   Ibid., p. 161.

by people who have been bitten and in the treatment of epilepsy, arthritis, cancer, polio, and high blood pressure.

One day, only 17 years old, he went to collect venom from the vipers and was fatally bitten.

It happened as Kuki had feared it would. After many months of grieving, she still chose not to run away from Africa. She wrote, "The love of (her son's) life had been his death: but it should not also be the end. Even if he had physically gone, his spirit lingered, and the place and I were still there."[27] She imagines that if he had grown, he would have gone to university and returned with innovative techniques for "keeping the balance between the wild and the tame, learning the secrets of Nature and applying them to its protection and balanced development....

"The average urban African has never seen an elephant; how could these people make a policy which would enable them to protect the environment and at the same time ensure their survival? Was all the wilderness destined to disappear through lack of knowledge and planning?"[28] As a result, she established the Gallmann Memorial Foundation and used her ranch for research and development of many preservation projects. This she was able to do, despite living the nightmare of her son's death.

While Kuki's story shows triumph over dread and disaster, people throughout the world have taken their fear, fascination, and awe of snakes and made snakes into objects of cults. Just as today people tattoo snakes on their skins, people of the past wanted to capture the power of snakes for themselves. Not only snakes' ecological, but also archetypal history dwells in the recesses of our psyches.

In pre-Christian cultures the snakes' sinuous glide was seen as the epitome of grace and elegance, its skin marked with beautiful patterns, its eyes mesmerizing. The way it can inject venom through its bite made it a transmitter of knowledge and death. Its ability to coil and strangle was strength. A snake was a wise, powerful, healing ally.

---

27. Ibid., p. 250.
28. Ibid., p. 251.

Seen as the force of life itself, the snake was associated with women. In Paleolithic cave art, ca. 40,000–26,000 B.C.E., we find goddesses portrayed with the head of a snake and body of a woman. In Greece, ca 6,000 B.C.E., the bodies of sculpted goddesses were striped like snakes and entwined with snakes. The double spiral, a common symbol, represented the serpentine path to wisdom. Their penetrating gaze represented the all-seeing, all-knowing aspects of the deity.

In Egyptian culture, the word "goddess" is expressed by the image of a cobra. The goddess Neith appears as a golden cobra and was associated with weaving, which in turn suggested fate, the weaving of the threads of life. In a legend she brought forth the great god Ra, then took up her shuttle, strung the sky on her loom, and wove the world. Snakes crown the head of the goddess Isis as a symbol of her power and wisdom.

Especially well-known are the snake goddesses of Crete, ca. 16th B.C.E., found at the temple of Knossos. Wearing a tiara of snakes, these women look out piercingly. Their robust breasts are exposed and their skirts bordered with a net pattern like snakeskins. A snake is held aloft in her hand, or undulates up the goddess' arm and shoulders and down the other arm; another snake loops across her apron and wraps its tail around her ear.

The Omphalos of Delphi, long considered the center of the world, is conical in shape and shrouded with the net snakeskin pattern. A serpent Earth Mother coils around it protectively.

But, when patriarchal influences entered the Greek pantheon, the Gorgon Medusa was made to appear hideous and frightening. The legend is that having offended Athena, her hair was turned into snakes and she was made mistress of death's gate. This Medusa's gaze could turn one to stone (cold, closed-minded). Perseus kills her and gives her head to Athena, who nevertheless saw fit to wear it on her breastplate for powerful protection.

The aborigines of Australia believe that in the beginning the land was flat and that Rainbow Snake rose from its navel; with its mighty tail sweeps, it carved the landscape's mountains and water holes. Rainbow

Snake is synonymous with Mother Nature, and all her offspring have the responsibility of caring for each other.

In Mexico there is Coatlicue, the Aztec Mother of the Gods, which shows a double serpent head set upon a human body. Even today among the Huichol, when a woman sets out to weave, she first strokes a snake, then passes her hand over her brow and eyes to absorb the creature's beautiful design and power.

In the Chinese oracle, I Ching, hexagram #1, The Creative, is represented by a serpent who is light-giving, active, strong, and of the spirit, signifying success from the primal depths of the universe. For the Chinese this serpent is as electrically-charged and arousing as the force of a thunderstorm.

In India and the Far East the serpent image represented the spiritual concept of "kundalini," the universal energy that lies coiled as a snake at the base of the spine with its tail in its mouth. Rousing the snake through the chakras (the seven body centers of perception) by yoga and meditation, up to the crown of the head, the energy explodes into a flower of cosmic consciousness.

Many cultures venerated snakes by constructing landforms called serpent mounds. One of the largest is to be found in Ohio, built by the Adena people ca. 1000 B.C.E.–700 C.E.. At the summit of a hill, it winds a quarter of a mile; seven deep curves unwind from the tightly coiled tip of the tail to the head where open jaws hold an oval shape like an egg.

The transitional Judeo-Christian era introduced negative attitudes toward the serpent. In order to destroy the goddess culture, the male religious leaders denigrated women and snakes, turning both into evil tempters. But even as the Old Testament books were written, the snake was still a common religious symbol among the tribes of Israel. The connection of the snake with a tree or wand of knowledge also persisted.

The snake archetype still exists in the Caduceus—the wand of power encoiled by two serpents—which is an ancient symbol for healing. Buffie Johnson, author of *Lady of the Beasts*, writes:

The Serpent Goddess survives today as the medical Caduceus of the medical profession, its rod representing the Tree of Life. Originally a wand with three budding leaves, it became the symbol of the god Hermes, and in Greek myth the emblem of health and happiness. Adorned with garlands, it was believed to induce a state of trance and could be used to call up the spirits of the dead. It also became the emblem of the late demi-god, Asclepius, the healer.[29]

The snake resides in another powerful healing image—the uroborus, or the snake with its tail in its mouth. Here the open feminine mouth holds the phallic tip of tail and creates a symbol of wholeness. Shown to be "one" by virtue of flowing into one another are male and female, beginning and end, sickness and health, life and death, the oneness of all.

These are some of the cultural myths and images that may be referred to in dreams and visions. Further research into the specific image and its culture enhances understanding of the dream's overall messages.

DREAMS & VISIONS OF SNAKES

Snakes appear in our inner lives when our consciousness has become severely detached from our natural instincts, which can happen when we "do our duty" too much or live according to precepts handed down by parents or other authority figures. They come to balance the situation when we feel weak, when we are too much taken advantage of or dominated by others, when we lack self-determination and vital energy. To such situations snakes bring shrewdness, perception of what is really going on beneath surfaces, and the ability to slither around big obstacles. They also can indicate big changes beyond the range of our influence or willpower.

Often when snakes appear, people will feel afraid to get near the snake. As one woman said, "it always seems as if it is going to bite me and no matter what I do, it bites me anyway." The fear usually comes from some

---

29. Buffie Johnson, *Lady of the Beasts* (New York: Harper & Row, 1988), p. 191.

belief that has kept the person victimized. People inwardly cower before realizing the dimensions of their power, so it is good for them to be bitten by it even if they don't want to be. As with the wolf, the closer you get to the snake, the less fear and more power you will bring to your life. Endure the tension, let yourself be bitten, and face your vital issues, gaining the chthonic wisdom of the snake. As you accept your new-found values, the image of the snake in your dreams will be much friendlier.

Vicki Noble, a healer, has devoted considerable time to restoring her relationship to snakes. Part of that process has been the keeping of a pet boa constrictor. In her book *Shakti Woman*, she describes how after five years of intentionally living alone, she fell intensely in love with a new man. She immediately dreamed of <u>stumbling into the nest of a giant cobra, who strikes at her heart.</u> As Vicki awakened, she felt a sting in the center of her chest, and understood that her old self was dying and that kundalini energy was being awakened in her. To further explore the meaning of this dream, she went to an aquarium to visit a giant reticulated python. She relates that usually he was coiled and resting, but this day he roused himself and looked at her eye to eye. She felt the python was communing with her kundalini energies, which were swirling up and down. She says, "I was engaged in a deep struggle with my emotional and nurturing needs, while trying to figure out how to make a sufficient living. Then she had a dream, which she writes:

> helped me more than all the thinking in the world: <u>I am standing on wet red clay which suddenly begins to move. I realize it is alive and I feel threatened. I hastily attempt to get away, climbing up a huge cliff as fast as I can as the red clay turns into a huge red snake. As I look back over my shoulder, the red snake has become much larger and has turned white. It towers over me, laughing a huge, deep belly laugh (male), saying, 'When are you going to let me take care of you?'</u> On awakening, I feel so totally held by the universe that I am able to stop worrying and begin the always-necessary process of letting go in faith. Again the tangible presence of this totem made my life easier to handle by giving me

an irrefutable and direct contact with the natural world and its cosmic forces.[30]

The dream image of a snake's jaws wrapped around another creature may refer to the incorporating of another's being into oneself metaphorically. "Incorporate" means taking the corpus/body in. If we take in the spirit of another person and make it part of us, we may be more tolerant of others.

On the other hand, a dream of a snake's sinuous body wrapped around another may suggest that one is being squeezed or squeezing another so that the dreamer or the other cannot breathe. There is too much pressure. Someone is being smothered or devoured. Many of us have asthmatic symptoms and bronchial-lung illnesses, such as pneumonia, that threaten to squeeze the life-breath out of us. Because our bodies send warnings in dreams, the situation causing the symptoms needs remedying. Or, what seems overpowering needs to be removed. So much of the meaning depends on the personal context and what the dreamer feels to be true.

For instance, a therapist described how when she was working with a man imprisoned for 20 years for sexual assault and burglary, she asked him to close his eyes, center his attention on his belly, and see if he saw an image there. A snake appeared. He was about to express his contempt, when he saw the snake coil gently around his body until it completely enfolded him like a cocoon. He felt filled with a sense of comfort and safety, and he realized that this was the first expression of love he could recall ever having received in his life.

The snake's shedding of its skin universally symbolizes resurrection, immortality, regeneration, and creativity—creativity as the process of moving from old spaces to new—dying again to be reborn. We too shed the cells of our skin, although it takes seven years. We also shed relationships and jobs, when the form no longer fits. We cast off old selves and slip away like the snake in a new form.

A woman, for example, at the time of selling her house, where she'd lived for 20 years, was sad to leave her community of close friends and

---

30. Vicky Noble, *Shakti Woman* (San Francisco: Harper, 1991), pp. 121-3.

organizations and came upon a shed snakeskin. In that synchronistic moment, she felt confirmed in her decision to move. She realized that the old skin had been comfortable and safe, but it was worn and had lost its sheen. Identifying with the snake helped her make the transition slowly but surely.

Snakes know how to cruise about and adapt to all sorts of conditions—wet, dry, underground, forested, stony. They like to bask in coiled repose, absorbing the warmth of the sun. "Full-functioning with no superfluous part," poet Virginia Adair wrote in a poem called "God to the Serpent." Worldwide archetypes, they've been revered as shamans and the primal energy of creation and reviled as one who speaks with forked tongue and tempts with the knowledge of evil. Regardless of how they've been interpreted, these ancient beings, so different from us in their ways, want us to draw close to them, to be known as they really are, to be remembered, to coexist with us.

In conclusion, here are the thoughts of the contemporary Native American, Linda Hogan, author of *Dwellings* and other books. She wrote that her father could smell reptiles from a distance and keep horses away from rattlers. Her respect for snakes strengthened when

I dreamed of a woman who placed a fantastic snake over her face. The snake was green and the woman merged with it, wearing it like a mask, her teeth fitting inside its fangs, her face inside its green beaklike, smooth-scaled face. They became one. Her breath became the snake's slow breathing, and they lived through one another, inhabiting a tropical world of wet leaves, vines, and heavy, perfumed flowers. As the woman began to dance, other people emerged from the forest wearing feathers, deep blue and emerald green, like human birds brilliant with the dew on them. They joined the snake woman in a dance, placing their hands on one another's waists the way Chickasaws, my tribe, sometimes dance. Everything became alive with the movement of that dance. But after a while, the music became sadder than the jungle, and both disappeared a bit at a time behind the large dark leaves, vanishing behind rain into o the rich, fertile song of water. The woman removed the snake and placed it on a wall where it hung alive and beautiful, waiting for another ceremonial dance. The woman said, "All the people have pieces of its skin. If they save the pieces, it will remain alive. If everyone owns it, it will be preserved.

At first I thought this dream was about Indian tradition, how if each person retains part of a history, an entire culture and lifeway remains intact and alive, one thing living through the other, as the snake and woman in the dream. But since that time, I've expanded my vision. Now, it seems that what needs to be saved, even in its broken pieces, is Earth itself, the tradition of life, the beautiful blue-green world that lives in the coiling snake of the Milky Way.[31]

---

31.   Linda Hogan, *Dwellings* (New York: Simon & Schuster, 1995), p. 138-9.

INSECTS AND SPIDERS:
THE WONDERS OF THE SMALL

In Every Stitch of the Web

Insects comprise the largest class of animals by far, with tens of millions more said to be unidentified. Of the known species, beetles number about 40%, prompting author Sue Hubbell to quip "We do not live in a Nuclear Age or an Information Technology Age. We do not live in a Post-Industrial Age, a Post-Cold War Age, or a Post-Modern Age. We do not live in an Age of Anxiety or even a New Age. We live in an Age of Flowering Plants and an Age of Beetles."[32]

Insects have a hard outer covering and a body made up of three segments—a head which bears a pair of sensory antennae, a thorax with three pairs of jointed legs and often two pairs of wings, and an abdomen. Spiders' bodies have two distinct parts—the cephalothorax (combined head and thorax) and abdomen, which are separated by a waist. They have four pairs of seven-segmented legs. Spiders also have glands that produce venom as well as silk.

Edward O. Wilson sums up their importance in *The Diversity of Life*:

Entomologists are often asked whether insects will take over if the human race extinguishes itself. This is an example of a wrong question inviting an irrelevant answer: insects have already taken over. They originated on the land nearly 400 million years ago.

---

32. Sue Hubbell, *Broadsides From the Other Orders* (New York: Random House, 1993), p. 41.

By Carboniferous times, 100 million years later, they had radiated into forms nearly as diverse as those existing today.[33]

Aside from the preponderance of the small, the keys to their success are the ability to metamorphosize, organize, and adapt. They service life on this planet like no other. Without insects and spiders, plants would not live. Swarming over every patch of the Earth's surface, they often exist in symbiotic relation with other living beings. Without their labor, our Earth would be deluged with tons of decaying leaves, corpses, and feces. Nutrient cycles (nitrogen, oxygen, carbon, water) would be blocked.

Insects have been engineered to fit into the tiniest niche—from the canopies of trees to the bottom of the oceans. Make yourself small and step outside and this is what you will find if you have the eyes or equipment to look: insects in every nook and cranny of flowering plants, consuming them for their own life, as well as pollinating them for the plants' reproduction. Springtails, spiders, centipedes, and beetles turning the soil around the plants' roots and decomposing dead tissue into nutrients required for their growth.

Stoop by a river or stream and watch dragonflies catching their prey on the wing and darting to defend their section, water striders skittering across the surface, sucking up juices from dead insects. Water boatmen swim under the surface of the water, rowing along on their backs, using their large rear legs to push. Small black whirligigs spin around, using one pair of eyes to look above the surface and another pair to look below. The detritus of fallen leaves are devoured by the larvae of caddisflies, stoneflies, midges, and mayflies that breathe through gills and turn the vegetables into meat. The presence of these creatures is the best indicator of the water's health and cleanliness.

Closer to home, inspect the skin of your pets and your body, and you will find mites on hair follicles and sebaceous glands. Despite the walls of our rooms, cockroaches, spiders, centipedes, flies, moths, beetles, and fleas find their way in.

---

33.   Edward O. Wilson, *The Diversity of Life* (Cambridge, Mass.: Belknap Press, 1992), p. 210-11.

Insects' fantastic designs suit them for multiple roles in the food web. Some predators, like ladybugs, eat aphids. Insects provide high-protein food for birds, moles, and many other animals, including humans. Black flies may annoy us but they are essential for pollination and as food for bats and birds. Many parasitic mites, fungi, protozoans, and nematodes would not be able to survive without them. This is why ecologists point out that no scavenger, symbiont, predator or prey can be removed without ripple effects throughout the entire ecosystem. Such partnerships rule the kingdom, on which the rest of us depend.

Insects can be small because they don't have lungs as we do but trachea that diffuse outside air quickly through their bodies. Their spinal cord runs bellyside instead of along their back. Butterflies taste with their feet, crickets have ears on their knees. A form of metamorphosis enables them to grow out of their external rigid skeletons. Bees, butterflies, and beetles change form by going from egg to larva, to pupa, to final form. Others, such as katydids and water striders, hatch out of eggs, looking very much like adults only smaller. As they mature, they break from and step out of their former shell into a larger model.

Some insects' bodies are entirely sensitive to light; they are in a sense all eye. Many have single-lens eyes on the tops and sides of their heads that complement the vision of their iridescent compound eyes. A lovely example is the eye of the goldeneye lacewing, which has a background of black topped by a six-pointed star, shimmering blue at the tip, followed by green, then yellow, with a red center. Compound eyes, which are made up of many individual "eyes," perceive many different images. They see colors, especially toward the ultraviolet end of the spectrum, but most are missing red. Especially sensitive to movement, they see patterns invisible to us. Bees see the blue of the sky as shifting angles of polarized light that can be read like a map and interpreted. If an insect species' vision is less good, they likely will have longer antennae. Antennae enable them to be very sensitive to air movements, smells, and vibration.

An amazing communication feat of honey bees is how they determine the whereabouts of a food source or site for a new hive. As Karl von Frisch described in *The Dancing Bees*, after a foray outside and back in the hive, a she-worker does an arabesque dance involving figure eights, speed, repetitions, accounting for the position of the sun and winds. As she dances, other workers watch closely, keeping their heads close to her body and touching her with their antennae. In this way workers receive clear instructions about where to go. Contrary to popular belief, most of the approximately 5000 native bees in the U.S. forage and pollinate on their own; they live underground, not in a hive with its division of labor.

To us it seems many insects have infamous mating habits (but playing the comparison game, you find parallels in our species). Males often go to great lengths to ensure that their sperm, and theirs alone, will fertilize the females' eggs. To isolate their partners, the daddy longlegs puts a cage around his mate with his legs until she lays the eggs he has fertilized. A certain male dragonfly has a blunt penis, which he uses to squash down any other sperm in the female so that his will stay on top, in position for fertilizing the eggs. A damselfly has a spiked, bristly penis with which he can scoop out any competing sperm. Some male dragonflies keep their grasp on the back of the female's head after copulating, guide her to an egg-laying spot and hold her there until she has done so. Others hover near the female and drive away other males. The female *Parnassius* butterfly, white wings with dusky black edges marked by brilliant red spots, is mated with soon after she pupates for about three hours. She can only mate once because the male secretes a fluid that solidifies over her reproductive opening so only his genes will be passed on. If the male doesn't hold on correctly in copulation, the cap won't form; if he holds on too long, he'll be locked to her forever.

Spiders do marvelous things with silk. Relying on at least 3000 sensor points, they can build webs within an hour, even on water. Many can cast long threads into the air and be carried far and wide by the wind. In this way they have spread and repopulated barren areas. In 1883 the island Krakatau, located near Sumatra and Java, was destroyed by a series of violent volcanoes, leaving only a lifeless remnant of the island. A year later one tiny spider was the only sign of life, presumably having arrived by air. Soon the plankton of the sea and wind and rain-carried seeds and spores and other insects would arrive to weave a new ecological web. Wherever an ecosystem is damaged by fire, storm, or manmade disaster, spiders are among the first to start recreating life.

Ants epitomize the way insects have learned to synchronize relationships that function exceedingly well. Ants carry their food home to share with their extended families or colonies. Their society generally consists of wingless female workers, winged males and winged virgin females and a queen that may lay millions of eggs over decades. Workers rarely breed but focus on care of the colony—building and repairing the nest, gathering food, nurturing eggs, and tending the youngest—the helpless white grubs. They clean the grubs and fight off infections in three underground kingdoms with antiseptics from special glands.

Ants form partnerships with other animals and plants. Herdsman ants get their food as sugary droplets passed as excrement from tiny insects that suck juices from young leaves or unburst flowers. When the insects are done, the ants carry their wards to new pastures. A plant's hollow stem provides a home for the ants; it also produces starchy nodules to feed them. In return the ants protect the plant from enemies, such as beetles. Up to half the wildflowers in American woodlands are planted by ants. The flowers produce pods which fall and burst open or leave their seeds directly on the ground for the ants to pick up and carry home, beneath the ground. The ants feed their young and put the chewed seeds in compost heaps, ideal for germination.

Leafcutter ants offer perhaps the most remarkable example of diversified labor. You can see them in a South American forest, in lines with each carrying a segment of leaf from the tree canopy to their nest. Each ant travels day and night, running the equivalent of a marathon with a 500 pound weight. The leaves are brought home, where sets of ants reduce them in size and finally masticate them, then set the pulp down, where a fungus is formed that the colony feeds upon. Many plants and trees rely on fungi growing at the base of their roots to take up needed nutrients from the soil. The ants pamper it and keep it clean. Also in hollowing out the chambers 15–20 feet below ground for the nest of the eight million ants in their community, the workers move, aerate, and fertilize more soil than earthworms.

Ants can be ruthless killers too, combining force of aggression with numbers. One particular African ant (the driver) is the most fearsome of all. These ants live in colonies of up to 20 million partners, operating as one army with many tentacles. When they march, they've been known to kill tethered horses and human babies; they've been used to execute criminals. Resemblances to the battles between raiders and defenders are certainly found in our societies.

While we get alarmed by seeing colonies of ants or swarming bees, we could respect their risk of death. For instance, bees do not sting while collecting pollen or nectar unless they are stepped on or attacked. When they sting, the stinger is pulled from the bee's body, eviscerating it. Because they die after stinging, they will be careful to use that certain death-act only in defense of their hive, its honey, and sister bees.

The true nobility of insects lies in the work they do for the Earth, not just themselves. We, on the other hand, create food and habitat for only our kind. It may well be that insects and their devoted maintenance of life, is what makes them more likely to survive than us.

Bugs and Us

Stephen Kellert, professor at Yale, published a book on *The Value of Life*, in which he describes the results of a study of human attitudes, feelings, and beliefs about animals and nature. He defines nine values and then shows how different groups relate to them (e.g. according to gender, age, urban & regional demographics). The values briefly are distinguished as

utilitarian—seeing animals' use for food, medicine, clothing, tools
aesthetic appreciation—admiration for their beauty and the world's unity
dominionistic—exercising control over wildlife
ecologistic—understanding the relation of organisms and habitat
humanistic—affection for and bonding with animals
moralistic—concerned with respect and ethical treatment
naturalistic—interest in being outdoors

symbolic—use of animals in communication (literature) and
thought
negativistic—avoidance and dislike

Among many conclusions, Kellert found that rural people have more
dominionistic attitudes, tribal people more utilitarian values, and urban
people more moralistic. When people receive more education, their
ecological values increased. He also found that "the majority of Americans
failed to appreciate the extent to which the intellectual quality, emotional
value, and material well-being of their lives depend on an abundant,
healthy, and diverse living world."[34] He says that since our tendency to
affiliate with animals is not as hard-wired as our instincts to breathe or
feed, affiliation must receive enough social reinforcement to become
engrained in our culture.

Since our perceptions about individual species affect the laws we pass
regarding them, a species' destiny depends a great deal on people's
knowledge, experience, and values. The most disliked animals of all in his
study were the cockroach and the mosquito. Of insects in general, only
butterflies and bees seem to have redeeming features in our eyes. The
reasons many people dislike, even loathe, insects are their strangeness,
multiplicity (seems out-of-control), and indifference to us. They come
into our homes uninvited, sting us, exposing our rot, and often drive us
crazy.

Those who ignore insects' worthy contributions focus on how they take
away our crops, flowers, wood, fibers in clothes, and crumbs of food. Yet
studies prove that in an unspoiled habitat, insects eat no more than 15%
of plant material, leaving the ecosystem no worse off. But, when humans
take over grasslands to grow food for themselves—corn, wheat, rye, rice
and millet, they alter the landscape by creating unbalanced monocultures
with plenty of fertilizer and stored seeds lying around, which attract insects
in droves. In this way we've made it easier for ourselves to get Lyme disease
from deer ticks, for fleas to colonize dogs and cats, or for insects to
congregate in greenhouses. In an attempt to get rid of insects at any cost,

---

34. Stephen Kellert, *The Value of Life* (Washington, D.C.: Island Press, 1996), p. 63.

we have spent $3.5 billion a year on an arsenal of weapons, mostly poisonous, to eradicate so-called "pests," but we haven't eliminated one species yet and often harm other wildlife.

Rachel Carson's *Silent Spring* (1962) issued a wakeup call about the damage that the first round of synthetic chemical insecticides were causing soil, water, wildlife and human health. Since then more effort has been made to develop safer controls on the nation's agricultural lands. People experiment with a number of options to pesticides—biological controls, rotation of crops, variation of planting times, companion planting, and limited, targeted spraying. Increased ecological awareness has led to plenty of experimentation with viruses, protozoa, fungi, and bacterium (*B.thuringiensis*); the matching of a pest species with its predator or parasite, and the trapping of the males of a species and sterilizing them so they won't produce offspring. If we were more tolerant of fruits and vegetables with blemished skins, our produce could be less toxic.

Insects' homes are also affected by our elimination of forests and wetlands. Declining populations of pollinators, especially bees, wasps, butterflies, moths, flies, thrips, and beetles, mean plants are not setting seed as much. Wetlands purify drinking water, protect us from floods, are home to fish and waterfowl, but in the lower 48 states we have destroyed more than half of our original supply of wetlands (an estimated 120 million acres out of 215 million), and no let-up is in sight. In fact only recently have people begun to view wetlands as other than disgusting breeding holes of annoying insects that bred malignant diseases.

Another danger has been the practice of collecting dead specimens. Between 1983 and 1992 a ring of butterfly poachers, pretending to be botanists, allegedly captured protected butterflies from Western parks, forests, and wildlife refuges. When busted (the first such example in history), the ring had 2,375 specimens with an estimated value of $307,642, representing 14 of the 20 butterfly species listed under the Endangered Species Act.[35] Many butterfly collectors, including museums, ignore the fact that the specimens they take may be illegal. The trouble is

35. Ted Williams, "The Great Butterfly Bust," *Audubon Magazine* (New York: March-April, 1996), p. 30.

that collectors prefer their specimens dead and don't want restrictions on their hobby. The rarer a species, the more avidly they pursue it.

With flagrant disregard for butterflies' right to life and freedom, collectors scheme to regulate the life stages of the butterflies and obsessively order and label their conquests. The home of Richard Skalski, a pest control operator at Stanford University who was one of those arrested, was discovered to have chrysalises hanging from the ceiling over his bed to admire. His practice was to take the newly emerged butterflies as soon as their wings had become pumped up with blood and hardened for flight and store them alive in glassine envelopes in the refrigerator. Tom Kral, also arrested, had collected since childhood and said that his motive was "the joy of finding and documenting something new and different. Aesthetically, I like looking at butterflies; I find them beautiful."[36] On one of his trips he described filling 9000 envelopes with butterflies. One might hope that when he was arraigned, he felt something of what it was to be a netted, pinned and labeled victim.

Other people have responded to the beauty of butterflies differently— by creating gardens for them. The new popularity of attracting butterflies has risen like birding did 100 years ago. Clubs, zoos, magazines, and Internet sites also facilitate butterfly watching and photography, which increase knowledge and help stave off extinction.

Scientists and business people value insects for their utilitarian purposes. Medicines may be derived from insect chemistry. Spider's silk helps make fishing nets. Bees' honey, royal jelly, propolis, and pollen have been used in beauty and healing products, since history was recorded. Some healers now replace acupuncture needles with stings from live bees, claiming that for chronic ailments, such as arthritis, they jolt the immune system into stimulating the adrenal glands to produce cortisol, a natural cortisone. Venom is used for pesticides. Fruit flies are studied in regard to human memory and aging.

Our world needs more entomologists, those who can look into the microcosmos, to learn from it, and advise how to protect it. We tend to

---

36. Caroline Alexander, "Crimes of Passion," *Outside Magazine* (Santa Fe, N.M., January, 1996), p. 30.

empathize more with vertebrates, the animals like us, forgetting we are kin to insects too. Water fleas reproduce through live birth, as we do. Their hearts and digestive systems are vestiges of our own. Insects create tunnels as conduits for nutrients that are like the circulatory systems of our bodies. The way decomposers break down matter reflects the processes of our digestive systems. We all share the fact of death. But insects do more— they can turn death into life.

DREAMS & VISIONS OF INSECTS

James Hillman, the archetypal psychologist, has written an intriguing essay, called "Going Bugs," about how insects affect us psychologically. The word "bug" comes from "bugge" or "bough," which in the Anglo-Saxon past meant a terror, ghost, or devil. "Bugaboo" and "bogeyman" further that association. The word "bugs," Hillman reminds us, has long been part of psychiatric language. "Going bugs" refers to people's skin-crawling hallucinations and obsessional worries. The "bug house" is where they end up if their symptoms get too bad. (In computer lingo we have adopted the word "bugs" to refer to what's wrong. That's because in actuality a bug crept into the first large-scale computer and ever since we have been trying "to get the bugs out.")[37]

When bugs appear in dreams, they are at first likely to be met with aversion, anxiety, and dread, reflecting the dreamer's conscious attitudes.

A typical example is from a woman who dreams that in her garden her cabbages are being destroyed from within their stems by black borers. She tries to squash them but they are hard to find and keep up with. This typical dream shows how resentments, envies, and other insecurities eat away at our insides and are very hard to get rid of. They, like cabbage borers, will destroy the plant, the outer growth, the nourishing fruit. Allowed free rein, they will ruin the garden. Plucking is not adequate. Probably as in good organic gardening, the bed must be prepared in a way that deters borers in the first place. Generous applications of manure equal

---

37. James Hillman, "Going Bugs," *Spring: A Journal of Archetype and Culture 48* (Dallas, TX: 1988), p. 43.

generous expressions of angers, hurts, and griefs, which transform into beneficial humus. Supplying the soil with nutrients, not starving it or working it too hard, is comparable to treating our bodies with good nutrition and rest.

Once I had dinner with a man, whom I'd known briefly years before. At the dinner I grew very enthusiastic about him and apprehensive about what the future would bring. That night I dreamed that <u>we were eating from a bowl of insects like cockroaches that were coated with purple syrup. But when the insects got too big we were too repelled to eat them.</u>

A decade later I can say that that image summed up the history of our relationship. We had intense talks for years, laced with erotic love. His being involved with someone else became the too-big insect we could not eat. I tried for years to bite into this problem but could not do it. The cockroach stayed whole and substantial in the bowl before us.

In dreams and images a common motif is that insects enter through a hole, suggesting the vulnerable place in a person's protective containment or defense. They wound us to get our attention. "Hives" are both homes of insects and an irritating nervous inflammation of our skin. The inner arms are particularly affected, those soft surfaces that embrace, hold and hug. Our ability to love and be intimate is a problem to many of us. When we dream of parasitic insects, the implication is that we are acting like parasites, taking in all work, affection, friendship without giving anything back. Insects often show us what is buried or repressed.

Our first reaction is usually to get rid of them. A man dreams of <u>insects on ceiling, which seem to be dancing or fighting. I take a broom and crush them and wipe away the spot so that the ceiling looks all right again.</u> In doing so he tries to restore everything to blankness, the status quo.[38]

When in our dreams and outer lives large masses of insects keep coming at us, we can be certain of some disharmony between mind and the body's systems. Because insects represent an early stage of evolution, they may seem more alien, even though they are part of our beings. By accusing them of raiding our kitchens, destroying our crops, we make them scapegoats for our own ways of proliferating, dominating, poisoning, and

---

38. Ibid., p. 56.

taking over the planet. It is we, not insects, who pollute rivers, soils, air. We need to make a great effort to see our selves as the marching fire ants of our dreams and to come to terms with this understanding.

In doing so we can become more open and receptive to insects, letting them aid us. The scientist E.O. Wilson, whose work has been so devoted to ants, considers the following a recurrent nightmare because it expresses his anxiety about ants' being wiped out and his feeling of not doing enough work for them:

I'm on some fabulous tropical island like New Caledonia, and my plane's about to leave. Suddenly, I realize I haven't collected any ants. So I get back in the car and I'm driving, driving. I know there's a great forest on the northern side of the island, but I can't seem to find it. It's getting later. So I start looking for some trees, but all I can find are subdivisions. The land has all been developed. I can't find a single ant.[39]

Dreams are personal narratives, myths cultural. While everyone looking at ants, bees, spiders, or butterflies sees them from their own perspectives, past cultural myths can expand insights into our own behavior and time. When such archetypal images appear to us now, we may be especially electrified.

In pre-Columbian Mexico a legend arose about a worker ant that planted a seed from which all people developed. All over the world ants commonly are known for their tough will and doggedness no matter what the conditions. King Solomon praised the industry of ants in the sixth chapter of Proverbs. In China they typify good citizenship—clean, patriotic, virtuous.

In Greek and Roman myths ants represent the instinctual organizing mechanisms of the unconscious. In the many versions of the tale about Eros and Psyche, the young woman is given the task of sorting an enormous pile of myriad seeds by morning or face execution by Aphrodite.

---

39.   Elizabeth Royte, "The Ant Man," *The New York Times Magazine* (July 22, 1990), p. 39.

The conscious mind of Psyche is overwhelmed. But in the night the ants come to her rescue and do the job, illustrating the realm of order deep within us.

Once upon a time the spider bound the Earth together. In the Hopi Indian mythos, Spider Woman saw the empty silent earth and mixed earth and water from her mouth (saliva) to make the first humans. She taught the art of weaving on a loom of sky and earth cords, the warp stick of sun rays, the heddles of rock crystal and sheet lightning. Indebted to spiders, Indians made their crafts of spinning and weaving a high aesthetic priority. Navajos today put a hole in their baskets and blankets to represent the spider's burrow.

In West Africa the spider's thread represented an umbilical cord between God in the sky and humans on earth. The spider's silken thread is tied to the divine. Among the Hindu spiders were known as the spinners of fate.

Spiders weave in a spiral, a form that is sacred, because the center is connected to the outer rim of the circle. The spiral is used in dance and healing to illustrate the evolution of change. The web is like a mandala, the symbol for the wholeness of the psyche.

Spiders also ceaselessly build and destroy. In nature and our lives the flux between beginnings and endings, the old dying away for the new, is constant. We must continuously sacrifice what we have built in repetitive transmutations throughout the course of our lives.

Transformation is the main theme of butterfly dreams and myths. In Japan butterflies are associated with a girl's blossoming into a young woman.

The sense of divine rebirth associated with butterflies has been poignantly used by Haitian adults during extreme war and poverty. As parents have stood on the streets with their children with no food or homes, watching people they know get killed, they have instructed their children to think of butterflies, as if that vision was the best hope they can offer. The metamorphosis of butterflies tells of the soul's immortality after death.

Being in the chrysalis is like the necessary time a soul needs to be shielded from the world. The writer Kazantzakis said that one of the most memorable lessons he'd received in his life took place when he found a chrysalis and rashly decided to pry it open. The prematurely hatched butterfly could walk but not unfold its wings. It was doomed. Kazantzakis learned from his visceral grief about the importance of timing and letting nature do its work—whether in the creation of intimacy, deepening a work, or healing the body. The organic process needs to be patiently deferred to.

"Busy as a bee" is a common expression. When we feel at one with a task, we are like the purposeful bees. The constant hum of their wings is like eloquent song to those who work closely with them.

In Greece bees were likened to souls. Bees swarm from the divine source and made golden honey—out of sunlight—for the gods and goddesses. Temples were shaped like hives with "melissae" (bee maidens) as attendants. A swarm of bees appearing around the mouth indicated honeyed (soulful) words. An abundance of nectar implied poetic enthusiasm. When the pollen pockets were empty, madness and confusion resulted.

In the Old and New Testaments, land flowing with milk and honey meant fertility and abundance. The interaction of flowers and honey—bees do their pollinating, then transform the nectar into a pure, unalloyable substance—is a marvel of the ecological web.

An excerpt from Antonio Machado's poem evokes how the soul makes use of past experiences that may seem like failures and transmutes them into sweet rich nourishment.

> I dreamt I had a beehive
> here inside my heart.
> And the gold bees
> were making white combs
> and sweet honey
> from my old failures.[40]

---

40. Antonio Machado, *Times Alone: Selected Poems,* tr. by Robert Bly (Massachusetts: Wesleyan University Press, 1983).

Insects, these miracle workers, who can turn death into life, should not be repulsed but made friends with. They are the cosmic connectors and transformers. Looking into their enchanting stories, it seems as if the Creator packed the biggest force in the smallest package.

DEER: MARTYRS OF THE WILDWOOD

Proud, Aloof, Starving

The word "deer" means "shining fire" in early English,[41] perhaps because deer carry themselves on long, legs that leap like flames. Once upon a time their ancestors had five toes on each foot, and then via evolution the first toe disappeared, the second and fifth toes diminished in size, moved to the rear, and became dewclaws, while the third and fourth toes enlarged and hardened into hoofs. Deer trot long distances over hard ground with heads held high, bounding gracefully and easily over high obstacles. Tucked in their narrow, sinewy legs are vital glands for marking the ground and enhancing sexual attraction. Bucks and does curve their bodies and entwine their legs so that they can urinate on the hair tufts covering these glands. (Perhaps ballet dancers copied deer in the way they bend and twist, moving on hard toes with heads lifted and long-legged stature?)

Ancestral deer were known some 20 million years ago in Europe and Asia, then diversified and spread onto this continent via the Bering Strait. At that time they lacked antlers but had tusks. Eventually antlers evolved from short stalks to an array of tines and forks. The largest deer that ever lived, the "Irish Elk", in his prime was seven feet tall with a span of antlers up to 14 feet. Now N.America houses only five species—moose, elk, caribou, white-tailed deer and mule deer—with two distinct subspecies of blacktail deer. Whitetails in the East live in wooded river bottoms and

---

41. Buffie Johnson, *Lady of the Beasts* (San Francisco: Harper & Row Publishers, 1988), p.216.

valleys; mule deer in the West dwell in open, brushy country and high mountain terrain; blacktails live along the Pacific coast.

Antlers accentuate the pride of deer. They are both crown and responsibility, as they must be grown and shed every year. Making them depends on a nutritious diet. Soft knobs in the spring, as they grow the antlers look like velvet, while they are covered with a furry skin that protects the blood veins inside the antlers. At this stage the bulls have to move carefully amidst trees to avoid damaging their antlers. By early fall the soft cartilage has turned to very hard bone. The velvet loosens up and starts to fall off, which itches the bull, so he speeds the shedding of the velvet by rubbing his antlers on tree trunks. By mating season antlers are bright and hard, their size determined by the age of the deer and how well-nourished he is. A white-tailed deer's antlers are fine and branched, while a mule deer's are more blunt and forked. A moose's may be palmate with small prongs projecting from the borders, often compared to upturned hands. At the onset of winter the antlers have to be discarded. Males knock them off by hitting trees. The discarded antlers become good sources of calcium and phosphorus for rodents and carnivores.

As browsers, deer seek nutritious plants and face hazards different from carnivores. By the time they are eight or nine their teeth can get worn down to the gums, making it hard for them to eat and then they starve. Winter is their hardest time because then their metabolism rises and their need for food increases. Sparse vegetation from drought or fire also weakens them.

Deer prefer to feed in daylight but have learned to move about at night to avoid people. About dawn, deer set forth to munch on leaves, grass, and twigs for an hour or so. Chewing their food only long enough to swallow it, it enters the first of four stomach compartments. They then find a safe place under cover for the majority of the day, such as a ridge, from where the scent of everything that passes wafts up to them from below. There the swallowed food is returned to their mouth in amounts they can chew thoroughly, sometimes while lying down. When the food is swallowed again, it goes into the third and fourth stomach compartments where it is acted upon to provide nourishment for the rest of the body. In late afternoon, deer venture out again for another feeding session.

Because white-tailed deer tend to congregate together near their birthplace out of habit, they are more vulnerable to starvation when the resources become scarce or they've overpopulated an area. Mule deer are less so because they will migrate to distant regions to find food. Moose, because of their intimidating size and ability to forage alone, feel safe enough to linger in their home territory. To some extent herding is protective because some members can always keep watch for coyotes, bobcats, cars, and other dangers.

As people have moved into the open fields where deer forage, deer have learned their way around our homes, as many of us know all too well, having seen certain garden and farm crops bitten clean off and ruined for the season. People also dread being bitten by their ticks and getting Lyme disease.

Deer face severe problems as a consequence of humans interfering with the balance of populations in ecosystems. For example, once upon a time a particular mountain range could have held wolves and deer, and the wolves kept the number of deer in check, but when we extirpated the wolf, a vicious cycle was set in motion: the deer population soared, they stripped the vegetation, and then starved. The mountain range would take decades to recover and in the meantime be littered with the bones of deer. (Aldo Leopold wrote a famous essay about this situation, called "Thinking Like a Mountain.")

Another type of interference: Some people have trapped elk and started game farms for profit. The elk are captured when they wander onto privately owned lands, where regulations don't reach, and then fees are charged for hunting. A guided hunt to tourists, for example, on Ted Turner's Flying D Ranch in Montana in cost about $8500 for trophy elk, $3500 for mule deer, $3000 for white-tailed. Some game farmers have introduced more dangerous tactics. They steal prime elk from public lands, cut off their velvet antlers and sell them to Asians, and subject the elk to breeding practices that are likely to render them extinct. For instance, game farmers have brought in European red deer to build their herds faster, Texans cross elk with mule deer. In hybrid offspring of red deer and elk, the red deer's characteristics dominate, and yet red deer don't fare well in extreme cold as elk do. The hybrids perish, leaving the breed weaker.

As people "manage" the populations of species on particular lands— introducing this one, removing that one—"wildness" becomes more and more compromised. The presence of deer napping in our backyards makes this abundantly clear.

Controlling Fire

For all their shared history humans have mostly regarded deer as prey and hunted them. The quick lithe deer have tried to leap out of our way and live freely. Just as flickering flames of a fire refuse to go out, so they continue to elude us.

The connection between "pray" and "prey" is interesting in regard to the theme of hunting. To "pray" is to petition God or make an offering to the gods. It is a law of nature (God) that we eat "prey" to survive. For many cultures the act of hunting and eating another was done in a sacred manner with a sense of sacrifice. A challenging hunt was also supposed to strengthen one. Deer made eminent martyrs to this cause.

The history of hunting is virtually synonymous with the history of deer. Let us take a brief look at the varied attitudes for what they say about ourselves in relation to deer.[42]

Ancient people's hunts were accompanied by rituals and sacrifice, which they believed would alleviate their guilt and prolong the life of the species. Tribal cultures used deer fully—their meat for food, their skin and bones to make clothing, shelter, blankets, fishing lines, needles, scrapers, and ornaments. In Paleolithic cave paintings deer are depicted with reverent majesty. The stags have antlers with branches that crown them like rays of the sun.

The ancient Greeks considered hunting an epic act and the deer an important symbol of heroism, as can be seen on their marvelous vases. The

---

42. Matt Cartmill, "Hunting and Humanity in Western Thought," *Social Research*, (New York: New School for Social Research, Fall 1995): pp. 773-786.

early Romans denounced the Greek model as overblown. For them hunting was an ordinary farm chore, and deer were flighty cowards. But theirs was the first culture to manifest <u>anti-hunting</u> sentiments.

The Bible depicted a mixture of beliefs, which are still around today. On the one hand, humans were viewed as the corrupters of the hallowed Garden of Eden; on the other, they have dominion over all the creatures. The forest is a hell full of animals that terrorize people, as well as a peaceable kingdom. (However, John the Baptist and other hermit saints declared that animals were kinder than people.) Animals are lowly, animals are sacred. Jesus was born in a barn and attended by animals. He is quoted in the Book of James as saying to a multitude, "How much better than you are the beasts which know me and are tame, while men know me not."[43]

Before the 10th century, small farmers hunted more or less freely on their own land. But as new techniques of agriculture produced a surge in crop yields and population, the forest was cleared by ax and plow to make more farmland available. The aristocrats then increasingly usurped hunting rights, putting the remaining patches of land off-limits to peasants, thereby keeping the lands for themselves as royal hunting preserves. Hunting thus became an elaborate ritual of the elite. The peasantry, who were punished for taking game, developed heroes such as Robin Hood, a celebrated hunter who robbed many deer from the rich to give to the poor.

From the 11th–14th century deer were idealized as the object of a noble hunt. Language reflected the deer's elevated position. Deer territory was labeled "wild-deer-ness." The words that meant "animal" or "wild beast" in several European languages narrowed to mean "deer" or "doe" (e.g. English *deer*, French *biche*, German *Wild*).

In late medieval and Renaissance art and literature down through the 16th century the deer hunt also became a prominent metaphor for erotic love. Deer were so magnificent and vulnerable, so easy to sacrifice. The death of a noble stag became a tragedy. A crucified Christ was often depicted as a hunted deer with a cross between his horns. A compelling image of the time was Albrecht Durer's drawing of a severed head of a stag

---

43. James 3: 7-8, King James Version; Cartmill, p.777.

with a crossbow bolt in its skull and its eye turned backward to look at the guilty viewer.

In 1511 Erasmus denounced hunting as "bestial amusement." Thomas More echoed his sentiments in *Utopia*. Others claimed it was a form of oppression to peasants, although nobody said it was oppressive to <u>deer</u>. Shakespeare almost always portrayed hunting as murder, usurpation, or rape. For instance, in *Macbeth*, Macbeth's slaughtered wife and children are referred to as "the murder'd deer."[44]

Montaigne wrote that "foolish pride and stubbornness" made people set themselves before other animals.[45] While hunting had been attacked partly to rebel against the upper class, people had also grown to think about animals differently, since many farmers then lived and worked side by side with them. They shared an affinity that was quite different from the awe the cave artists felt.

The scientific revolution of the 1600's and the next three centuries further eroded the animal-human distinctions. When animals were perceived by humans as more than non-rational automatons and thus deserving of moral consideration, anti-hunting sentiments increased. In the 18th century animal suffering prompted teachings on being kind to animals.

Today people are still divided over whether hunting should be extolled or condemned. Polls indicate that most Americans agree that hunting for sport or for trophies to mount on a wall, or for any other purpose than meat, should be illegal. But, polls do not solve the matter. The controversy over hunting covers many issues, beyond the scope of this book. The top reason usually given for hunting is enjoyment of the outdoors; indeed hunters tend to know more about wildlife than anti-hunters. They find food tastes best when they are fully responsible for obtaining it. One such hunter, David Petersen says that he

Loves the freedom they embody and the primal adrenaline rush their musky animal essence sends surging through my soul. And

---

44. *Macbeth*, 4.3, lines 205-6; Cartmill, p. 779.
45. Montaigne, *Essays*, 2.12, "Apology for Raimond Sebeond"; Cartmill, p. 780.

I kill elk in order to bring their strength into my body, their beauty in my home, their wildness into my heart. I hunt elk in order to be elk.[46]

The most spiritual of hunters crave participation in the cyclic unity of nature. Ted Kerasote writes in *Bloodties*: "He gives me this place, my strength, and I like to think that someday my bones will fertilize the grass that will make his grandchildren fleet."[47]

In this debate I feel I owe you my position. When I was a teenager, my stepfather introduced me to b-b gun shooting. I practiced with it. One day I actually shot a nutrea that hung on a fence after a flood. In the instant the bullet hit the animal, I felt my heart break. I never shot another creature since, nor wanted to. I respect the feelings expressed by Frank Waters in *The Man Who Killed the Deer*, in which he writes about a native American modern male, who has lost touch with the traditions of his tribe and has been disturbed by guilt over his deer killing. At the end the man lies at night under the stars and reflects:

The Deer were up. He watched them twinkling in the immemorial, indestructible pattern against the inky blue. There were the long-stemmed legs, the upflung antlers. There was the pointed nose and the lifted tailpiece...And he knew now there is nothing killed, nothing lost, if one looks far or deep or high enough to see how its transmuted meaning is imprinted for all men [sic] to read and understand.[48]

Many of us prefer to "hunt" deer with our eyes, our cameras, our sketching pads, and in our meditations. Let us remember that deer do not

---

46. David Petersen, *Elkheart: A Personal Tribute to Wapiti and Their World* (Colorado: Johnson Books, 1998). As stated in *Northern Lights*, David subsists mostly on roadkill.

47. Ted Kerasote, *Bloodties*, (New York: Kodansha International, 1993), p. 176.

48. Frank Waters, *The Man Who Killed the Deer* (Athens: Swallow Press/Ohio University Press, 1942, 1970), p. 265.

threaten us. Too often in relation to them we put our own wants and plans before consideration of them. It's time to find a win-win solution so that they do not always have to be the victims. For the fact remains that from ancient times to the present, deer resonate with meanings so intense that the sight of them will bring us to a halt on the road and hush our voices.

MYTHS & DREAMS OF DEER

The buck with the crown of antlers looms out of the bare trees, exciting the mind's eye. His tan arched neck gracefully supports his triangular head. His big eyes look into ours. He is noble, still, and watchful. Infusing this simple image in a dream or vision is an atmosphere of commanding majesty, one that has been felt deeply since humans observed deer.

White deer and female deer bearing a crown of antlers have been especially numinous because of their rarity. Biologically the appearance of antlers on females only occurs among reindeer but psychologically a dream that brings the two sexes together suggests unity within the self. Because antlers are shed and renewed every year, they commonly symbolize regenerative powers. But they've also been described as wings, rays of the sun, and spiritual antennae.

Just as deer rub their antlers against trees in a kind of dialogue, so we press their qualities in search for inner truths. Deer possess a delicate tension, for instance, and because they quickly spring away, they teach us about backing off from control, letting something or someone be free. Lovers know this spring well; building trust takes time.

The impulse to control a person or situation is usually caused by fear. To restrain from control feels like standing in the heat of fire. But containing the fire within ourselves is the better way. Freud, Jung, and later depth psychologists recognized how containment of our emotions facilitates inner transformation. A literary example of this dynamic is Dante, who when he was denied a relationship with a young Beatrice, poured his feelings into a work that became *The Divine Comedy*. The principle applies equally when beloved children leave home and much as it may hurt parents not to advise them, in the end both parties are more likely to attain a respectful bond if we let them make their own choices.

The strength of the male has fascinated humans for eons. In *Animal Guides* psychoanalyst Neil Russack describes the case of a man who had been born to a clan of people, who for generations had lived by the North Atlantic Ocean.[49] Circumstances were such that he was given up by his mother for adoption. As he matured—after many business successes, affairs with women, and prestigious honors—deep within himself he remembered a wild vitality he had once but now felt walled off from. Then he dreamed of an elk that he fed upon as if it was the most important meal he'd ever received. This detail points back to a time when people ingested the animal as a homeopathic sacrament, believing that in so doing, they acquired its physical, moral, intellectual, and divine power. In the man's dream, the eating of the elk signified a new sense of self-empowerment. He began a search for his actual parents. When he found his kin (his father had died), he had this dream: <u>A full-sized elk appears. I look into the mirror and see an image of me.</u> Seeing himself at one with the elk took the earlier dream a step further, giving him an ecstatic sense of renewal. Identified with the elk, the man regained unity of strength and purpose in his life.

Bull elk or bucks have been connected to the powerful, even supernatural energies inherent in sexual desire. After musing on the presence of a deer at dusk, D.H. Lawrence felt his inner stag appearing and wrote in a poem entitled, "A Doe at Evening:"

> Ah yes, being male, is not my head hard-balanced, antlered?
> Are not my haunches light?
> Has she not fled on the same wind with me?
> Does not my fear cover her fear?[50]

As Lawrence's poem hints, the female deer, in contrast to the masculine, possesses vulnerability and sweetness. The doe's grace has inspired numerous art works, from Greek vases and the Bayeux Tapestries to the

---

49.   Neil Russack, *Animal Guides*, (Toronto: Inner City Books, 2002), pp. 125-9.

50.   John Hollander, ed., *Animal Poems* (New York: Afred A. Knopf, 1994), p.95.

appealing mother of Bambi. The female is often associated with the gentle receptivity of the soul, so needed for both men and women in our fast-paced business-oriented, materialistic society.

In *Man and His Symbols*, edited by Carl Jung, Jolande Jacobi describes the case of Henry, a reticent, bookish, 25 year old engineer. In part of a dream he walks along a willow-bordered brook, enters a wood, whereupon a doe runs away. Jacobi writes: "The wood is a symbol of an unconscious area, a dark place where animals live. At first a doe—a symbol of shy, fugitive, innocent womanliness—emerges, but only for a moment…The man who fears the communications of his inner depths (like Henry) is as much afraid of the feminine element in himself as he is of real woman. At one moment he is fascinated by her, at another he tries to escape."[51] It's important that he realizes that the doe represents a way he acts toward himself first. As such a man becomes more at ease with actual women, his psyche will reward him with a dream in which the doe does not run away but may in time teach him more about the nuances of love.

An important characteristic of deer is that they do not travel in a straight line in their perpetual search for nourishment and shelter. We might reflect on the deviating paths we too must take through life, using our intuition to make decisions or coping with what fate brings us. The unknown future often appears like entering a dark wood. The deer, crossing our threshold in a dream or vision, may invite us to follow—that is, perhaps to enter wild-deer-ness or embark on a new adventure.

Thus, pursuit of the deer can be a form of answering the "call," the first step of the hero's journey, as Joseph Campbell has depicted so well in *The Hero with a Thousand Faces*. He writes:

> Whether dream or myth, in these adventures there is an atmosphere of irresistible fascination about the figure that appears suddenly as a guide, marking a new period, a new stage, in the biography. That which has to be faced, and is somehow profoundly familiar to the unconscious—though unknown,

---

51. Carl G. Jung, ed., *Man and his Symbols* (New York: Doubleday & Company, 1964), pp. 281-2.

surprising, and even frightening to the conscious personality—makes itself known; and what formerly was meaningful may become strangely emptied of value.[52]

So it was with the young prince Gautama Sakyamuni, whose father sheltered him from any familiarity with the world outside of wealth and pleasure, so that he would inherit the throne without distraction. However, the gods arranged for the prince on various excursions to see an old weak man, a diseased one, a dead man, and then a monk. The shocked prince felt the call to retire from the world and eventually would become the Future Buddha. Another well known call came to Mary, who in the Gospel according to Luke, had the vision in which an angel appeared to her and told her that she would bear a son given to her by the Holy Ghost. Her humble, obscure life was forever changed.

The "call" is not only about establishing a new religion. Every parent who brings a child into being, especially a mother who carries it in her body and endures the ordeal of giving birth, answers a call and crosses the threshold to a new life. The "call" can also be experienced as a vision of a new art work, the need to move across country, or the design of a garden.

The hunt can be viewed as a metaphor for the next steps and the difficulties or good fortune along the way. Having begun as the answer to the voice of the spirit within, often in the midst of struggle and despair, the quest leads to the actualization of as yet unrealized potential. Meditating on one's dreams and following the leads of one's personal imagery take one on this journey.

A period when the myth of the hunt expressed sacred values was the Middle Ages. Hunting ceremonies were then governed by courtly rules of romance and chivalry. The British tales about King Arthur and His Round Table of knights and ladies often involve the pursuit of a deer. Sometimes the deer is called a "hart;" it is not difficult to infer that the King or knight is chasing his heart's lead. In one story of Sir Thomas Malory's *Le Morte d'Arthur*, King Arthur runs his horse to death in pursuit of a hart and in a

---

52. Joseph Campbell, *The Hero with a Thousand Faces* (New Jersey: Princeton University Press), p.55.

dreamlike state, he meets Merlin, who foresees his demise at the hand of Mordred. A chain of events leads to the hunt for the Holy Grail.

An interpretation of this story is that following one's heart contains the seed of one's destiny. One fulfills the seed of Self by taking the paths inspired by the inner spirit, and sacrifice may be required. The pattern repeats, but every pilgrimage with its spiritual treasures and every destiny are unique though. The many stories about the quest for the Grail are at the center of the Western mystery tradition.

While the Moon-goddess Artemis has been linked to the hunt, pure water, and the virgin forest, she has also been the protector of deer and often shown with them. The ancient Greeks called her groves "deer gardens." This story about Artemis illustrates the consequences of disrespect. One day while the goddess was bathing, she felt herself being looked at as an object, her privacy violated. Acteon was spying on her from the brush, disguised in deerskin and antlers. In punishment, Artemis turned him into a buck and made his own dogs chase and consume him. This story warns of personal assault. Acteon's putting on the antlers turned him into the Horned God, with the obvious sexual implication. Because he did not behave in a sacred manner, Artemis attacked him without hesitation. She made him feel what it was like for a deer to be pursued and devoured.

We can hear echoes of this myth in the following dream of a contemporary wife/mother/worker: <u>The deer is leaping across the field, and large patches of its flesh are torn off by pursuing dogs.</u> In associations the dreamer noted that dogs dwell in the suburbs (as she did) and are domestic pets. The deer is wild and free. Personally, she felt driven to exhaustion and deprived of any sense of innate vitality or grace; she was being torn apart by all the family and work demands on her. She could identify with the deer's life being threatened by encroaching human society. In the Greek myth described above, the dogs tear Acteon apart because he disrespected and violated the goddess; in the woman's dream, the dogs may represent the woman's disrespect for herself; specifically, the "goddess" part that is the Great Mother, the regenerative force of life. The sadness this dream brought to consciousness inspired the woman to make an important shift by supporting natural habitat for deer in her neighborhood and spending more time in wild places herself, in moments of much-needed solitude.

As the dream of the harried woman shows, deer images can show us where we have been injured as well as how our attitudes have hurt the larger family on Earth. A painting (or poem) is a dream given form, and deer are a beloved subject. Frida Kahlo, the Mexican 20th century artist, painted an image called "The Wounded Deer." It shows a deer's body pierced with arrows, causing blood to drip. The deer's head is her face; it has large antlers. Presenting herself with the strength and majesty of a stag, she identified with the sacrificial deer. In her life she combated numerous operations on her back, often wearing stiff braces, often unable to rise out of bed, and yet she painted memorable works that marked her trials. Her self-portrait might well express much about our relation to animals today. Since we are dependent on them, we are to some extent one with them. When they bleed, so do we.

Shamanic healers of the past and present have turned to deer to aid them in healing disease of body and disharmony of soul. Donning masks and garments to impersonate deer, they dance and chant, calling upon deer spirits to guide them into the Lower and Upper Worlds. The origin of our beloved Santa Claus whose sleigh is driven by eight reindeer may well be the shamans of Lapland and Siberia, who ate white-spotted scarlet, hallucinogenic mushrooms and danced to transform themselves into flying reindeer. Over time the shamans bearing gifts of wisdom would metamorphosize into Santa, donned in red and white robes, bringing us presents.

Keeping the deer inside us alive and well is a worthy spiritual goal for ourselves and world. That means contemplating its many aspects, heeding the call, crossing thresholds, avoiding martyrdom, and flourishing with all our gifts intact. May we know happy, fruitful days of being in the wildlands with the deer.

FISH: INQUISITIVE FLASHES FROM THE DEEP

Maybe you've thought how can I relate to fish—they are just too different?! But when we swim, we enter their world. Aided by snorkel or scuba gear, we can float underwater with our eyes open as they do. Fish swim up to us closely, not enough to touch, but to inspect. What do you suppose they see about us…?

Because our planet is mostly covered with water, astronauts who could clearly see the whole of it coined the name, Blue Marble, for it. When the first living cell appeared, as much as one-third of what is presently land was once under water. Early sea fossils looked like sponges and jellyfish. Tubular marine creatures gave rise to animals with a segmented body and a flexible spinal rod. Primitive fish, appearing about 500 million years ago, were the first vertebrate. Since we are vertebrates too, they are our ancestors. For about 40 million years fish developed rapidly. As the Earth suffered its various cataclysms—the worst 225 million years ago, the Permian extinction, when 96% of all sea life was wiped out—new growth was sparked that resulted in a tremendous variety of fish adapting to the abundant niches found in water.

The sea is more than our ancestral home. Water also composes our bodies in roughly the same percentage as water is to the surface of the Earth. Our blood even contains about the same percentage of salt as the ocean.

We humans spend our first nine months in fluids, growing as if in the sea. During this time the physical resemblances between us and fish are most evident. The microcosmic photographs of Lennart Nilsson reveal that human embryos in the fourth week show the precursor to gills below our heads. After two weeks, this pre-gill form grows instead into our lower jaw, larynx, and ear. We have vestiges of a tail. Where fins were, we developed arms and legs. Fishness is imprinted in our bodies and psyches.

The Fin Within

Fish are immensely important in the food chain and the health of all waters. They may seem too remote so far under the water for us to heed, but that is a tremendous oversight. We need them more than they need us. In order to appreciate them and the role they play in our inner attitudes, we need to pay attention to how they mate, raise their young, how they spend time alone and cooperate with each other, how they work out conflicts. From the grand panoply of species, in this chapter I will focus on some of the most popular—sharks, fish of the coral reefs, and salmon.

SHARKS

The first sharks appeared before dinosaurs and have remained remarkably much the same, while other fish changed enormously. Shark skeletons are made of cartilage, not bone. Their skin is thick and tough, rough like sandpaper. Their strong tail with the upper portion larger than the lower is an extension of backbone. We have named about 370 species and discover four or five new ones every year. The whale shark, Earth's largest fish, can grow to 60 feet while the smallest, the "tsuranagakobitozame" (Japanese for dwarf shark with long face) is only four-five inches.

These sleek, sea-colored creatures are found in waters all over the world. Born with teeth and the ability to swim, shark pups are ready to survive on their own after being born. Sharks take as long as us to reach sexual maturity. The sandbar shark delivers eight or nine pups every other year. Duskies breed every third year. If left alone, they can live 30 years.

Sharks usually keep moving, for when they are still, they must use more energy to get water flowing through their gills. Gliding with powerful fin action, they take in air at the surface of the water and hold it in their stomachs to keep themselves afloat. Oil in their liver helps keep them buoyant. They swim separately, except during mating season.

Sharks can go several months without eating. Like wolves, they prefer food that is easily caught, such as dead or weak animals. They have a sharp sense of smell. They see better in dim light so are most active at dawn or dusk. Through what is called a lateral line system that extends along body and tail, they hear and feel other presences. They also have special cells on their exteriors, so they bump up against a fish to feel if it would be good to eat. They do not sleep but rest on the sea floor or in caves with oxygen.

Most sharks have four rows of teeth. A new set grows every two weeks, pushing out the row in front. With their teeth, they bite and tear, not chew. They can reject undesirable food by turning their stomachs inside out. Sharks are often accompanied by pilot fish that depend on feeding on their scraps.

CORAL REEF FISH

No one knows why coral reefs produced such an explosion of fishes, so brilliant in design and color, but nearly 40% of the world's fish species dwell on reefs. Like flowers and butterflies, the beauty of coral reef fish dazzle in their inspired and playful designs. Purple and black angelfish, red coneys with blue polkadots, blue-and-yellow-striped grunts, cute blunt-nosed trunkfish with pursed mouths, energetic wrasses, rainbow parrotfish, sleek trumpetfish, schools of silversides, to name a few of the abundant variety.

Many animals on the reef dwell within the confines of another organism. The short goby shares a home with a nearly blind bulldozer shrimp. The goby guards, and the shrimp rests its antenna on the goby's body in order to sense vibrations. Some fish clean the skin, gills, and teeth of other fish. The fish are closely linked to productivity of the reefs built by live corals (tiny animals too).

One of the dazzling features of their sex lives is the ability of some types, such as sea horses and groupers, to change gender when the opposite sex is in short supply. (The same brain changes are involved in trans-sexuality in humans.) Razorfish and sand perch live in harems, consisting of one male with two or three females; these fish, plus sand tile fish, groupers, and others, change from female to male. If something happens to the lead male, then the next biggest fish, a female, makes the sex change over the course of two weeks. The new male then becomes the protector. The smaller females produce eggs. Males make sex changes too. In clownfish society, if a female is injured, eaten or grows too old to lay eggs, a smaller male turns into a female and produces eggs instead of sperm.

Many mysteries remain about the behavior of these fish, a good reason for caution in our treatment of them.

SALMON

Salmon evolved about eight million years ago and demonstrate the most admirable struggle for existence. Life begins where rivers are barely above the level of small pebbles. Three months after several thousand eggs have been spawned, only about 100 will hatch. The others may be defective or eaten by scavengers, a constant threat at every turn. The hatchlings remain in the gravel for another two or three months until one night they wriggle free and get a bit of air. When they have swallowed enough air to achieve neutral buoyancy, they can then swim instead of float. While in the streams, they are the color of the water with spots like pebbles.

But as they grow, they head toward the sea in search of more food. Depending on how much help they receive from high river flows of spring snowmelt, their journey may take a few days to several months. They become acclimated to salt water and their bodies adapt the camouflage of fish that roam the high open seas—dark blue-green back, silvery sides, and pearly belly.

Several years later and perhaps 2500 miles away, the urge to spawn triggers another remarkable journey back to freshwater and their birthplace, where they will procreate and die. Fish that have spread thousands of miles apart in the seas converge and arrive at their natal rivers within days of each other, guided by their olfactory senses and sophisticated internal navigation systems using the sun and Earth's magnetic field. When they come out of the salt water to the freshwater, they jump above the surface of the water, usually full-length or higher (some would say joyfully).

For their nuptials their bodies change dramatically again. Sockeyes' heads turn bright green, their torsos cherry-red. The males' backs hump, their teeth enlarge and jaws hook for combat. Their way will be blocked by many hazards: commercial fishermen, dams, predators. On the way they will stop eating. Only about two adults from the original 1000 eggs will make it back to spawn, and they will be battered and broken inside and out.

Yet the female will first vigorously dig a nest in suitable gravel. Her efforts attract suitors. The male courts by repeatedly touching her body. Eventually the pair will lie side by side with bellies close together near the bottom of the nest. Their backs arch, mouths gape open, eggs and sperm gush forth. The female will cover the eggs to prevent them from being swept away—for about two weeks until her death. And so begins and ends the life of the valiant salmon.

Controlling and Re-making Fish To Meet Our Wants

When people first discovered fish were good to eat, they built cultures around the cycles of fish lives, but they did not endanger fish populations. Strong tribal prohibitions safeguarded them. It is only recently that major fisheries have crashed all over the world, a tragedy not only for fish but also for people's livelihoods.

The problems are these: an exponentially expanded human population, technological advances in commercial fishing, unregulated exploitation, and pollution from an overwhelming amount of toxic wastes drained into oceans and rivers that not only destroys marine life but also has led to alarming hormonal changes. These deformities have been passed on to us and are known to reduce men's sperm counts and cause testicular cancer. The deteriorating health of ocean life profoundly affects the stability of the planet's weather and atmospheric composition as well.

Commercial fishermen have been able to use sonar, radar, and satellites to help them find fish. Huge ships spend months at sea, casting huge nets, called "curtains of death," that sweep up anything in their path. A terribly wasteful habit has been to throw away unwanted fish (about one-fifth of a catch). Many of these unnecessarily killed fish are juveniles, which would be much more valuable if allowed to mature. After a few decades of these practices the result has been a vacuum-sweep of the world's oceans. Many marine species (about 100) are on the endangered species red list, meaning that they are in peril of extinction in the next 15 years. Many other species are depleted, which means they could be recovered if all countries set policies to do so. So far the agencies and laws have not protected sustainability. In 1998 the first list of Overfished Species was compiled by the National Marine Fisheries Service, endeavoring to halt the depletion of fish populations *before* they became rare or endangered.

For decades movies and books humans have promoted an image of sharks as fierce and deadly, because some say the public loves having monsters upon whom fears can be projected. Sharks are seen as the "terrors of the deep" or "silent savages." The fact is, for instance in California, white young sharks use the warm coastal waters to grow up, and, if their lives are interfered with by humans, sharks will attack them. In actuality, humans threaten sharks by getting in their way. When people tread water, they resemble dead fish, easy prey in a shark's eyes.

The shark population has been decimated by humans who have harvested them for food faster than they can reproduce. Their slaughter is also driven by the Asian lust for allegedly aphrodisiac shark-fin soup. In order to render fins into noodles, Hong Kong imports billions of pounds annually. You can find shark cartilage pills in your local health food stores.

As for coral reefs, humans enjoy them on snorkeling or diving vacations. In doctors' offices tanks of tropical fish presumably keep people's minds distracted from their problems. Airlines show videos of coral reefs to calm fears of flying.

Meanwhile the reefs worldwide have been seriously degraded. Divers armed with bottles of lethal sodium cyanide chase reef fish into crevices and caves, squirt them, and soon fish swim dizzily out. If fish don't appear, the diver rips away pieces of live coral. The other unwanted fish sink or float away. Day after day, hundreds of tons of cyanide are poisoning reef systems, turning paradise into hell. Some of the captured fish are sold for fancy aquariums all over the world. The dead coral impoverish island communities, as it takes several hundred years to build them. To halt the destructive spreading "white pox" of coral reefs requires urgent action. Because when coral reefs go, fisheries follow, and then the food chain.

Human interference in the lives of salmon has disrupted their evolution. Everywhere except Alaska salmon are extinct or in grave danger. In the lower 48 states fewer than 10% of adult salmon are progeny of wild fish. Most are born and reared in fish hatcheries, highly industrialized production facilities created to grow fish. The needs of thriving salmon were sacrificed to the timber and electrical industries. Deforestation makes water warmer and more full of sediments—unhealthy for salmon. Damming rivers block their migration routes.

Some people thought fish farming might be the solution to the crisis in the wild rivers. Fish farming began innocently enough but as people experimented with management practices, blunders were made. First came the establishment of hatcheries. Then came selective breeding with its designs to increase fish eggs and their weight. The taste of farmed salmon is nothing like the wild.

Since in some places the management of fisheries is paid for by anglers' license fees and special taxes on tackle, exotic (non-native) species were introduced to lakes and rivers to provide anglers with more exciting sport. A big mistake, for in numerous cases they displaced natives by competing for food, eating natives' eggs or genetically swamping them in breeding. Half the endangered species are threatened by introduced fishes. Lake trout, for instance, eat native cutthroats at the same time they bully them out of their habitat. One-third of N. America's 850 native fish species were announced "rare" over a decade ago.[53]

Genetic tinkering and fish farms now dominate the industry. If this aquaculture advances, in the future we will see weakened, less nutritious fish and the bays and estuaries of the world turned into mazes of pens and ponds. Like Frankenstein, our experiments with fish have created more problems than solutions. This disrespectful relationship with animals surely needs therapy.

One problem is resistance to change, even though conservation makes economic sense by creating jobs and saving taxes. But if inspired people

---

53.   Jon Luoma, "Boon to Anglers," *New York Times* (November 17, 1992), p.C4.

returned to a relationship with fish based on gratitude and honor as the Indians once had, we and fish would be better off. With reverence and ecological insight, in the spring when the salmon were returning, the native people performed welcoming and preparation rituals, but no one was allowed to fish then. The fish would be allowed to pass safely to their spawning grounds, ensuring another round of life. This sort of "right action" was based on astute observation and recognition of a shared destiny. The first step toward change may be found in our dreams and imagination, where resides the heartfelt wisdom and courage to heal this broken relationship.

DREAMS & VISIONS OF FISH

Fish have appeared in art and ceremonies in all human cultures from the earliest times, because people were in awe of the vast waters surrounding them that teemed with life. Because the seas were so dark, mysterious, and deep, they came to symbolize the Great Unknown and all its contents—a.k.a. the collective unconscious. Fish though know how to navigate them with quicksilver grace.

Marie Louise von Franz, analyst and author and close colleague of Jung's, wrote:

> Psychologically the fish is a distant, inaccessible content of the unconscious, a sum of potential energy loaded with possibilities but with a lack of clarity. It is a libido symbol for a relatively uncharacterized and unspecified amount of psychic energy, the direction and development of which are not yet outlined. The ambivalence regarding the fish derives from its being a content below the threshold of consciousness.

In psychological theory, most of our life takes place in our unconscious, below the level of conscious awareness and rationality. So when fish are around in dream, we might look around for what new thought or insight is trying to surface. Fish, being flashes from the deep with keen senses of direction, have also been linked to intuitions. Because they swim easily, they are magnets for imagery about flow between upper and lower layers of consciousness, internal and external worlds, reason and emotion.

We know, for instance, how hard it is to achieve and sustain the sense of flow in relationships, whether between lovers or diplomats. Like fish, it is slippery, dies when trapped or hooked. The term "goddess of love" in Sanskrit refers to "she who has a fish as her emblem." (In dreams and art fish often appear iconic.) Love/eros is not just sexual chemistry but the harmony in talk.

If a fish in a dream involves a friend or lover, the dream often means something about needing more flow or intuition, permitting the fish to swim back and forth between you. A woman who wanted to criticize a dear friend's behavior dreamed: <u>We are walking together. There is a live fish swimming between us. I want to eat it. I pull off its tail and try to pull off its head. It becomes a live gory mess.</u> The dreamer felt warned—that in trying to catch the fish, dissect it (analyze her), she would in effect be killing the trust or understanding between them. She saw that if she spoke up she would make a mess of things. She decided to stay quiet until she could frame her thoughts more sensitively.

While dreams show us ways fish invade our personal consciousness, myths can expand our understanding by provoking us to think, muse, and question more about animals.

The earliest people were fascinated by the fecundity of fish. Those millions of tiny eggs carried within compact bodies. The precious protein and oils of their flesh. Thus, fish became sacred symbols of abundance, regeneration, and nourishment. In temples they were sculpted with jewels on their fins, lips, and gills.

The fish was the zodiacal sign of the first two thousand years of the Christian era and the symbol for faith in Christ. Jesus was the "fisher of souls," his followers "little fish." The fish is used in the Eucharist to represent the Christ's mystic body.

In Egypt Isis was portrayed as the Fish Goddess, shown crowned with a large fish (around 1500 B.C.E.) Ceremonies incorporated fish as representative of transformative journeys. Souls were immersed in the "sacred sea" and borne by fish through the dark waters. In funerary rites fish were believed to carry souls after death through the underworld. The waters of life were seen as the all-embracing "unus mundus" in which all differences were dissolved and made liquid. Paradoxically, waters regenerate life but also can kill through their all-consuming strength.

The Hindu god Vishnu was sometimes portrayed as emerging from the mouth of a giant shark. The Japanese storm god, "Shark-man," was a warrior who demonstrated his strength by swimming through the ocean with a shark under each arm.[54] As we know, the huge powerful sharks excite fears of hidden dangers. They are generally associated with predatory, voracious behavior—card sharks to corporate moguls who "play with the sharks." Because of cultural beliefs, when one has sharks in dreams, one has to see if one is dominating others or if beneath the surface an aggressive, ruthless attitude lurks. On the other hand, it may be that one needs to be more assertive in an adverse situation that could be destructive; or one is overly sentimental, attempting to escape a confrontation that is needed.

Salmon illustrate how to struggle against difficulties and vigorously participate in the major transitions of life. Like them, we are born, needing a safe environment. As we leave home to earn our living and mature, we change and adapt to new conditions many times over. Eventually we withdraw from outer activities to prepare for death. Although there are perils along the way, some of which take our lives young, ideally we will make it to a worn but natural end. For the Celts salmon and their life cycle represented the ultimate in heroism. Therefore they honored salmon and tried to learn from their ways.

The native people of the Pacific Northwest, whose lives depended on salmon, felt that they in a sense "became" salmon. When the salmon were caught, they were dried on sticks in the sun. The sun's rays became part of the salmon. When people died, they too were put on platforms, like the salmon, to become full of the sun.

A man dreamed, <u>I sat by the river, fishing. The river was flowing strongly from left to right. I hooked something which proved to be very</u>

---

54. Nicholas J. Saunders, *Animal Spirits* (Boston: Little, Brown and Company, 1995), p. 139.

heavy. I raised it to the surface and was horrified to find I had brought up the skeleton of a prehistoric fish, "something very ancient." This frightened me extremely. Usually the feeling of fright is because of the intensely numinous nature of the dream, the correct awareness that at a primal level confirmation of your fate is heralded. The river represents the continuous flow of unconscious imagery beneath the surface, from which the man is attempting to extract something. The prehistoric skeleton of the fish comes from the most ancient layer of the beginning of life. It represented an energy force and structure that powerfully affirmed his life.

In many healing stories, fish carry the person down to a deep-sea cavern where a wise figure, such as Neptune, is met. We may encounter bright playful coral reef fish. In their rainbow colors they represent psychic wholeness. They are like the precious jewels of spiritual process. They keep life beautiful and buoyant. They also often work in tandem with others.

Fairy tales often tell of a fish that emerges from the water to grant a fisher three wishes on the condition of secrecy. Usually fancy homes, wealth, and beautiful mates are wished for and granted. But then the fisher, persuaded by others' greed, succumbs and reveals the source and is instantly cast back to his/her original state. The stories warn of avarice, pride, and disrespect for the sacred encounter.

Fish appear in our dreams to appeal for help in their own distress as well as to draw attention to our own. Many people dream of fish out of water, lying on the sand near death. The fish clearly needs help but there also is something inside us that is dead or struggling to flow again.

A therapist in Seattle, wrote about a 26 year old medical student—a bright, healthy attractive woman—who came to see him with complaints of lethargy, an inability to focus on her work, and gloomy thoughts. She said that one day she heard on the radio that the fish area off the east coast where she lived was nearly depleted of its harvests. She had been besieged by thoughts about the threats to the salmon, over-population, ozone depletion, greenhouse effect, air and water pollution, and how humans were causing their own extinction. The therapist said her depression had acted as a shut-down valve on her intense agitation over the threat of extinction. For this kind of depression some doctors will prescribe antidepressants. He chose to confirm her perceptions, assuring her that her thoughts and emotions were valid and appropriate. He advised her to get to know other people who felt the way she does, read books and get involved in activities.

He emphasized how giving this person medication would desensitize her and make her worse. Healthy people feel their culture acutely. He thought that she was like a canary in the coal mine. (If the canary died, the miners were alerted and exited the mine as fast as possible.) As a canary, she could show people how anxiety and stress were warning signals. This approach allowed her to outgrow her depressive symptoms. "To remain calm and unruffled while the human species extinguishes itself is not good mental health…Feeling stressed is a healthy, appropriate and above all necessary response."[55]

Like this woman, in the face of constant bad news, many of us think, "what's the use?" Once I listened to a group of Hopi elders say they were no longer educating their children because they believed the world was doomed. I felt anger and frustration that they would give up. That position seemed wrong. Forging ahead as best we can, even if we are in the dark, seems the better alternative, because solutions may come from any direction.

An ethical attitude includes fish in your sense of community. A practical thing you can do is take care of streams in your area: Fish need clean, cool water. A stream suitable for rearing young fish should have spots of protective cover (pools, woody debris, boulders, overhanging trees and brush), moderate summer temperatures, and plenty of insects for food. A good spawning stream should have gravel with free-flowing, silt-free water. Don't let a stream's flow be redirected because fish can become stranded. Don't allow the relocation of one fish to another place. Guard against the spraying of toxic chemicals on streamside vegetation. Don't eat fish that are not caught in a sustainable manner.

---

55.   Thomas Wear, "Stress and the Canary Syndrome," *The Ecopsychology Newsletter 5* (California: Spring 1996), pp. 1, 7.

It is no accident that a particular creature appears in our dreams or preoccupies our imaginations. Its qualities can be applied to your personal life but also lead you to take better care of that animal.

BIRDS: HARBINGERS OF HOPE AND INSPIRATION

How can we get out of our skins long enough to comprehend even briefly the lives of others? When we try to understand the viewpoints of any animal—and in this chapter those of birds—we immediately encounter uncertainty about a bird's birth, parents, conflicts, good times, health, loyalties, inspirations, and even dreams. Learning all we can helps fill in the blanks.

In the case of birds we can start with an overview of their place in the tree of life. Most taxonomists now believe that birds evolved directly from small, meat-eating dinosaurs. The fossil of the earliest clearly identified bird (Archaeopteryx) dates back to the late Jurassic period, about 150 million years ago, when birds at least coexisted with dinosaurs. This bird had a lizard-like tail, jaws with sharp teeth, and claws on the outer joint of its wings.[56]

Fossils of birds resembling cormorants, geese, and herons were found in the Cretaceous period 130 million years ago. The major proliferation of birds started 65 million years ago with maximum numbers attained about 10 million years ago. All birds have feathers but not all fly. The boost to flight came when a tuft of feathers developed on the thumb, which controlled airflow. Once birds could get airborne, they could dwell anywhere: ocean, shore, rocky cliffs, beaches, dunes, salt marshes, freshwater lakes, ponds, rivers, mangroves, forests of all types, alpine meadows, grasslands, pastures, deserts, big cities, residential backyards.

---

56. Virginia Morell, "The Origin of Birds," *Audubon Magazine* (New York: March-April, 1997), pp. 38-45; *National Geographic* (July, 1998), p. 90.

Territories of Birdsong

Since birds are embedded in virtually every ecological community, they are essential to food chains. They prevent outbreaks of insect populations, contributing greatly to the health and productivity of trees by eating insects that chew on leaves and pollinate plants. Their removing insects from buffalo, rhinos, giraffes and other animals helps groom them. Their guano enriches the seas; dropped into water, it supplies the nutrients for plankton which feed fish, which may in turn be consumed by birds.

To thrive and do their jobs, birds obviously need territory that is spacious and fruitful enough for them to feed, mate and raise their young. They have a difficult life because we have installed towers, wind turbines, electric power lines, and open oil pits in their way. They face wetlands that we have filled, shorefronts that we have lined. Their stopovers on migratory routes have been plastered with our buildings. Forests have disappeared. Pastures and hayfields that once were homes for grassland birds have been converted to fast-growing crops that are harvested earlier, thereby destroying birds' eggs and young. Collectors steal their eggs to sell illegally. In the last two millennia one fifth of bird species have been eliminated. "In 2000, an estimated 12%, or over 1000 of all known species of birds were considered under threat."[57]

All this, despite the fact that the presence of birds and their conversations make our lives more joyful. Those who've studied birds' phrases say that sparrows, juncos, cardinals, meadowlarks have a repertoire of about eight songs; a starling 67, a mockingbird 150, and a brown thrasher more than 2000.[58]

Feathers define the fantastic beauty of birds. Think of birds of paradise, for instance, with long flowing tails like satin sashes, ribbed bibs or fluffy epaulettes, delicate plumes arching back from the top of their heads, gossamer glowing multi-colored wingspreads. Or, the Resplendent

57. Richard MacKay, *The Penguin Atlas of Endangered Species* (New York, London: Penguin Books, 2002. Also see www.birdlife.net and www.redlist.org.

58. Bill Rankin, "A Song for Every Occasion," *National Wildlife*, (Virginia: Aug-Sept. 1996.)

Quetzal, pheasants, tanagers, bluebirds, Roseate Spoonbill, Peacock, Sandhill Cranes, hummingbirds, Common Loon.

Aside from a palate of feathers, birds have an amazing design that makes them light and tensile strong. Their bones are thin and hollow, their feathers like thistle. One of their most fascinating—and little understood—habits is to migrate long distances at signals from the season. While birds are born with a magnetic sense, they must learn to use it and set their "compass" to the North Star. Birds know when and where to go, mapping their way somehow from landmarks, position of celestial bodies, magnetic fields, smells, infrasound, and gravitational forces. Timing is crucial in nature's ecology (and our psychology). For instance, precisely in mid-May, between 500,000 and 1,500,000 shorebirds arrive at Delaware Bay from S. America and gorge on the eggs the horseshoe crabs have just lain (a single female may lay up to 80,000).

Some birds only migrate when they seek better weather and food conditions, but others are big travelers, truly citizens of the world. Warblers go from the jungles of Venezuela in January to Yukon forests in June, Golden Plovers from Hawaii to Alaska, Kirtland's warblers go from the Bahamas to Michigan. Arctic terns fly 22,000 miles from the Arctic to Antartica. Most birds fly at low speeds, e.g. 25 mph. Golden eagles and hummingbirds go 50 mph. Some swifts fly up to 200 mph. Usually they stay at 1000–5000 feet but can scale the Himalayas at 20,000 ft. Hawks, vultures, and albatrosses can soar for hours without flapping a wing.

Mating customs can be quite special. To attract females male bowerbirds of New Guinea will collect ornaments, build the most extravagant nests, dance with much bowing and squeaking. Their nests may be nine feet tall with fresh flowers installed daily (blue is the usual color). Males will plunder each other's nests for decorations. We've learned that lengthy courtship displays stimulate and synchronize male and female sexual readiness; whereas, actual mating happens quickly.

Even though a pair is monogamous, they won't necessarily stay faithful. Males and females alike know that they can produce more offspring by being unfaithful. Some, such as hummingbirds, don't bond with any one female, but try to attract and mate with as many as possible. His irresistible colors give him the wherewithal to have a harem.

A small bird is lucky to live 10 years, a large bird 20. The greatest number of deaths occur to babies who are vulnerable to attack in nests and may even be left behind by threatened parents.

These are some generalities about birds. Now for a closer look at the characteristics of three very different types of birds. Keep in mind that these features influence our perceptions, ideas, and myths.

CROWS

Crows can live virtually anywhere in the U.S. and Canada—woods, suburbs, parks, along rivers and streams lined with trees—because they scavenge well for all kinds of food. When they are born, they are tended by both parents. They play games together: tug of war with grass and twigs, sliding upside down on tree branches, drop-the-stick and fly down to catch it, rolling down a grassy hump. When older siblings are ready to breed (mating for life), they often establish territories in or near those of their parents. One crow was seen to have a nest about a mile away from her parents but every Friday afternoon would return to hang around with her parents for an hour or so.[59] Sometimes crows leave their home ground for a convivial gathering on a roost with others, making all sorts of sounds that remind us of coos, growls, and gargles.

Clever and opportunistic, they cooperate in attacks on prey or predators. One was seen biting an otter's tail with a fish in its mouth. When the otter dropped the fish, the crow's compatriots swooped down and grabbed it. They have also been seen pulling up unattended lines of fishermen and eating the bait or catch.

We consider crows smarter than other nonhuman species because they have the cognitive ability to shape tools according to a plan. They do more than just use available needle-like thorns to tease prey out of crevices of trees or rocks. They make some tools with hooks, others tapered with a

---

59. Jane Brody, "The Too-Common Crow," *The New York Times* (New York: May 27, 1997).

barbed edge, shaping them with their beaks, removing leaves and trimming off the bark. These they take with them to different sites.

EAGLES

Hail to the chief: Eagles with snowy white heads and large dark bodies. Eagles with claws that can seize a deer. Tawny eagles with mantles of feathers on their head and neck as well as legs. Eagles uttering sharp metallic cackles as they coast on thermals with a flat, seven-foot wide wingspan. When they go after prey, they tuck in their wings and swiftly dive. Before hitting the ground, they spread their wings and brace their tail fans to create drag. In defending their territory, they circle and beat their magnificent wings with exaggerated slowness.

Perched on trees and capable of seeing prey a couple of miles away, they wait and watch a long time, looking for fish, waterfowl, and small mammals. With their sharply curved beaks, they can find food in lean winter, even when fish are under ice. Sometimes they will harass ospreys for prey or scare off crows and vultures from a carcass. But bears or coyotes will not get out of their way.

Usually eagles mate for life. At the time of mating they will do a sky dance of soaring, looping, and plunging. They grab each others' feet and lock talons, rolling and falling until finished mating. Then they separate and do it again. In nesting, the male hunts for materials while the female designs nests. They build very large nests—five to six feet wide, two to four feet tall, in big trees near rivers or lakes—which are used over and over again for decades by more than one pair. They will also build alternate nests nearby in case they are in danger. In spring the female lays one or two dull white eggs. Both feed their young. The eaglets grow fast but are dependent on their parents for three months.

Eagles can live long but their low reproductive rate and interference by humans makes them vulnerable. In the 1950s their populations were decimated by pollutants, especially DDT, in water and fish. The buildup of chemicals caused eggshells to be thinner and weaker and to crack open too soon. A reduction in the use of lethal pesticides and active recovery programs have helped them to recover.

OWLS

Owls look stocky due to their large heads, fluffy plumage, feathered legs and feet. Their beautiful though subdued plumage enables them to roost on their favored perches undetected during daylight hours. They have large immovable eyes set in front of their heads and therefore must turn their whole head to look at anything not directly in front of them. They can turn their heads 270 degrees in either direction. Owls see perfectly well in daylight but have a high proportion of light-gathering rods that enables them to see five times better in the night than us. Of all birds they have the best hearing. Asymmetrical openings in their large ears allow them to tell which ear is hearing sounds and pinpoint the location and distance of sounds. Many hunt in the night, using this exceptional hearing.

Barn Owls, found throughout most of the U.S. in open country, farms and grasslands, have very long legs and a heart-shaped facial disc that is thought to reflect sounds to their hidden ears. Also the serrated edges on their flight feathers suppress noise and enable them to fly silently. They are cinnamon in color and have speckled breast and wings, feathers tipped in gray with longer legs than other owls. They make a raspy screech and series of clicking sounds. They often live close to humans because they follow rodents which follow humans. Contrary to belief, a Barn owl can kill ten times the amount of mice than a cat in a single night. Yet people often shoot them.

Screech owls (eastern and western) spend most daylight hours roosting in hollow trees. They are small with ear tufts and yellow eyes and plumage of reddish, gray, or brown streaks. Great Horned owls are 25 inches long, gray-brown with barring on belly and prominent ear tufts. They utter rhythmical deep hoots as they go about their business in forests, city parks, and suburbs, feeding on rabbits, rodents, minks, weasels, skunks, birds, snakes, cats, bats, frogs, fish, and insects.

Most owls do not migrate much so they get to know their territory well. The Screech owl and Great-horned owl live here year around. On the other hand, the Snowy owl and the tiny Saw-whet owl are winter visitors.

A Favorite of Ours

Of all animals birds attract the most of our attention. Studies show how much we are like birds biologically. In courtship, for instance, we dance similarly—with bows, advances, retreats, and changing of partners. We wear bright clothes like plumage to attract the opposite sex. We cast coy looks, strut, make wooing sounds and triumphant cries. Males and females rub wings/legs together. We repeat these actions until pairs withdraw together to mate. As in bird societies, males try to spread seed, females to get the best partner. Like birds, we practice monogamy, as well as polygamy and promiscuity.

People today still use the migration of birds as a sign for planting and harvesting their crops. Many of us even migrate south for the winter and north for summer like they do.

Perhaps because of their accessibility, birds have been the subject of more studies than other animals. Alfred Russel Wallace's fieldwork, discussed in *The Malay Archipelago*, and his contemporary Charles Darwin's study of finches on the Galapagos Islands as described in *On the Origin of Species by Means of Natural Selection* jump-started the concept of evolution. Birds' lives have provided numerous examples in studies of population and community ecology. Scientists have used them to investigate mating systems, role of kinship, communication, inheritance and learning, hormones, genes, brain maps, their adaptation to extreme conditions and unusual niches, navigation, and more.

A plethora of museums, societies, array of magazines and journals are devoted to birds. Roger Tory Peterson's guides, first published in 1934 and which by 1997 had sold more than four million copies, were hailed as "the most influential natural history accomplishment of the century." Today an estimated 60–80 million people do serious birdwatching—feeding them, going on trips to birding "hot spots," counting, censusing, and fund-raising. Many keep lifelists. American Birds Magazine says birders spend 14 billion dollars annually on gear, trips, products.

I once asked individuals in my local Audubon group **why** they are so obsessed with birds? The answers: "birds are like finding hidden treasure," "they are usually cheerful," "they don't mind your watching," "they are always there and easily observed in most open spaces."

In order to protect birds, many people have been involved in the making of mammoth organizations, the passing of legislation, and recovery efforts.

The National Audubon Society was originally begun in 1886, founded by Dr. George Bird Grinnell of Forest and Stream Publishing Company. At the time a situation had arisen in which farmers had noticed that birds were not eating the insects as much as they used to, because the numbers of birds had been noticeably reduced by poachers of feathers, nests, and eggs for women's hats. The organization was formed to educate about and lobby for birds. In the early days public opinion was so hostile to change that two wardens of egret sanctuaries were murdered. In time protecting birds also came to mean saving their habitat, which led to focus on forest and river issues, as well as the serious threats from global warming and acid rain. Today the organization has over 500,000 members, 1000 nature centers, 500 chapters in the U.S. and more in Canada and Latin America.

In 1990 the National Fish and Wildlife Foundation launched the Partners in Flight Program, which includes more than 125 federal and state agencies, nongovernmental organizations, and 14 companies from the forest products industry, that jointly discuss and act on priorities in research, monitoring, education, and management for the benefit of neotropical migratory birds. In their view, however, Congress never appropriates sufficient funds for the agencies to fulfill their responsibilities to prevent precipitous declines in bird populations.

DREAMS & VISIONS OF BIRDS

Many people, especially the lonely, sick, depressed, and/or imprisoned, have found being around birds inspiring and healing. The experiences of the Japanese writer, Kenzaburo Oe, winner of the Nobel peace prize in 1968, offer a moving example. Fascinated with the language of birds since childhood, he read "The Wonderful Adventures of Nils," about a naughty boy who communicates with wild geese, which made him long to understand the language of birds and fly off with his beloved wild geese.

Little did he know that much later he would have a severely brain-damaged son, who was not able to speak much. When the boy was four, Oe and his wife played bird songs all day for two years. The boy learned to hum, and later after listening to such sounds, composed wonderful music for the piano and flute. The doctors said that the hemisphere of their son's brain that controls speech was very weak but the musical hemisphere was strong. None of this would have been discovered if Oe and his wife had not acted on their intuition regarding birdsong.[60]

From the time people interacted with them, birds have been endowed with sacred traditions. Shamans transformed themselves into birds so their souls would fly to the divine source for instructions on how to heal. Birds symbolize transcendence over material life and release from fixed patterns, the bridge between the human world and the divine, Heaven and Earth. It was said that when the sun warmed a bird, it became active, like a person in God's light.

Birds' wings suggested the glory, beauty, sublimity, exaltation, favor or help from on high. A bird in flight pictured the soul enamored of its highest ideal in prayer and contemplation. American Indians believed that birds had wisdom because their soaring enabled a broad perspective, the ability to see the overall picture.

Birds have been extraordinary muses. Torrents of sketches, photographs, paintings and sculptures have been created about them. Throughout the ages birds appear from the Paleolithic cave paintings, Egyptian tombs, and Greek vases to art in Europe and Asia. Bird masks were made in tribal societies. In 20th c. sculpture Brancusi carved sleek birds in chrome and stone, capturing the modern zeitgeist.

In literature famous ancient works include "The Conference of the Birds" by Farid ad-Din Attar and Aristophanes' comedy called "The Birds." Birdsong is virtually synonymous with lyrical poetry. In the novel, *Birdsong,* by the British author Sebastian Faulks, the grisly impacts of World War I devastate the land and many lives. At the end the sight of birds in the trees, fluttering and chattering, offers a shred of hope to the

60. David Remnick, "Reading Japan," *The New Yorker* (New York: February 6, 1995), pp. 38-44.

very wounded that life will be restored. And Emily Dickinson memorably wrote, "Hope is the thing with feathers that perches on our soul."

Most of all, birds have inspired music. Wagner wrote an aria about owls, ravens, jackdaws, and magpies for *Die Meistersinger*. The cuckoo and nightingale are heard in Beethoven's Sixth Symphony. In Bizet's *Carmen*, the opening words are "Love is a rebel bird that no one is able to tame."

Birds became archetypal because they were once deities. In early human times eggs were especially valued because of the importance of fertility. From 27–10,000 B.C.E. goddesses were made to look like birds, with breasts thrust forward and enlarged buttocks that cradled eggs. The planet, in its continually giving birth to new forms of life, was considered a cosmic egg. Birds germinated and carried the essence of life and the universe.[61] Bird goddesses were also portrayed as spinners and weavers because of birds' skills in nest-building. In Ecuador and Peru people still paint birds onto their spindles.

Aphrodite was depicted on the back of a swan to associate her with grace and love. Now we have a love stamp with two swans on it. The eastern Indian deity of deities, Devi, is also shown on a swan. The interchangeable swan, goose and duck ancestered the Mother Goose tales.

For Egyptians, hawks came to stand for the portion of every soul called "ba," which referred to one's immortal spirit and outlasted the body. Egyptian deities were often portrayed with human heads on the body of a falcon. To have wings meant the ability to have ecstatic flights to higher realms.

Every bird has its special significance. Since I selected crows, eagles, and owls for special focus, I'll elaborate on some motifs in their imagery.

Many cultures respect crows for their intelligence and watchfulness. Their ubiquitousness reminds that sacred energy is always around. Their raucous caws warn of dangers. Their mimicking, clownish and provocative antics have made them also known as tricksters. Because they are black, they have received projections of melancholy and the soul's necessary descent into darkness (depression) before the coming to light of new potentials. Along with the vulture and raven, because they feed on carrion,

---

61. Buffie Johnson, *Lady of the Beasts* (San Francisco: Harper & Row, 1998), pp. 7-90.

they were a common symbol for death. Van Gogh's last painting was the flock of crows flying over a field.

A man beset by the death of his mother and then shocked to hear that his sister had serious cancer took long walks on which he frequently saw a crow. It would hop along a fence, staying with but always keeping ahead of him. He began to think of it as a spiritual ally, a sign that the "higher powers" were aware of him. His sister would soon "pass over."

In *Just Before Dark,* Jim Harrison tells how one day after he had put in long hours of frustrating work on a film script, "I felt quite literally peeled in body and mind. I dreamt of a crow I had stared at for a long time at my grandfather's farm as a child. The crow grew larger and I noticed that there was a silver belled harness around its neck. I got on and we flew to a sandbar in the Manistee River where we fished and bathed. He said she carried him out of danger "as if she were a black, feathered angel." From this dream trip he obtained much-needed ease and refreshment.[62]

Because eagles looked like noble heroes, they were associated with power and war. Some of those who incorporated the strength, courage, and penetration of eagles in their emblems include: Zeus; Vishnu, who in the Indian epic Ramayana, used Garuda as his divine mount after the bird stole the gods' immortality; Horus of Egypt, Mithra of Persia, the Viking Odin, King Solomon, military Rome, Napoleon, and the United States.

The ancient Aztecs believed that when warriors died in sacrifice, their eagle-god, Huitzilopochtli, fed on their hearts. In the 12th century their chief god told the exiled people to settle at a place where they found an eagle perched on a cactus eating a snake. This place became Mexico City.

Eagles are able to swoop down into water and retrieve food. This ability is like being able to dip into the unconscious and not be overwhelmed or inundated by it, but able to scoop out a bit of sacred nourishment. That eagles can swallow a snake means that they possess powerful snake knowledge too.

Eagles bring the strength to fight the inner demons of confusion, despair, jealousy, and revenge as well as the outer demons of competitors,

---

62.   Jim Harrison, *Just Before Dark* (Livingston, MT: Clark City Press, 1991), pp. 284, 315.

swindlers, and ignoramuses. Instead of doing harm to ourselves or others, we can use eagle energy to transform the situation. The eagles' strong toes show firmness, the ability to grasp powerfully. Their strong beaks cut, tear, and crush. Eagle energy is about using words incisively and having vision. They teach how to hover, dive when appropriate, and use the winds of life for our benefit. They also show us how to mate with thrilling excitement.

A woman was embroiled in a conflict with others at the office and dreamed of <u>an eagle telling her, 'You are in danger of becoming fat squishy pulp for predators.'</u> She took heed and acted. Because women frequently have trouble asserting themselves in confrontative situations, an animal ally can be extremely helpful.

One ignores the eagle energy at one's peril. For example, a man who abandoned his wife had a dream of <u>a big eagle pecking out his eyes and skin for dishonoring the father-spirit.</u> Here the man was being punished for lacking courage and honor. The linking of the eagle with the "father spirit" brings to mind the myth of Prometheus who was chained to a rock by Zeus for having stolen fire, his liver eaten by Zeus' eagle for defying authority. The dreamer ignored the message of his dream, continued to suffer and eventually developed an illness.

Where the eagle was associated with light, the owl was associated with dark night, mystery and graveyards. One medieval name for owl was "night hag"—a witch in bird form. The owl is still associated with witchery on Halloween.

Yet the owl's wisdom did not go unnoticed. The owl symbolized the Greek Goddess Athena. Owls were thought to possess clairvoyance and magic because they could hear in the dark so well and fly silently. The way its tufts of feathers look like ears but are not gave them a reputation for hearing what is unspoken. They can see what is hidden.

Owls teach how to quietly enter a place and go about your business. They accomplish tasks with timing and skill (not intimidation), constantly listening, watching and waiting.

A man, whose day was punctuated with wine at lunch, martinis before dinner, wine with dinner, brandy before bed, and who at intervals had blackouts after evenings of much alcohol, dreamed of <u>a drunken owl,</u>

teetering on the edge of a barn loft. Clearly if it fell, it would die. The dream made him realize how perilously close to the brink his drinking had taken him. It motivated him to stop and join AA.

In many bird dreams a wounded wing suggests an injury to your ability to get your ideas or spirit off the ground and flying. A nest of eggs implies creative ideas needing to be tended. Mating with a spectacular bird like a cardinal suggests acquiring dash and brilliance, the ability to stand out and be noticed. A woman who had low self-esteem was shocked to discover that she has a peacock with a fanned-out tail in her attic. After the dream she accepted that a majestic being dwelled inside her and could be exposed to the outer world. It helps to realize that to make a small but concrete act in the world as a result of the dream will cause a significant change for you and perhaps the animal if you notice it more.

A common motif is of a trapped bird that needs release or liberation. Many people whose lives have been lived within social bounds, feel that when they get between middle and old age, they want to live life in a new way, break free, go on a trip, move to a new place. A man watching Sandhill Cranes depart from Platte River declared, "I ached to follow them, to rise up on wings of my own, to fly with them to some wild and unbounded place."[63]

To work with bird imagery, you first need to learn all that you can about the particular bird. If it coasts on thermals, see how you can use the natural currents in your life more. If it migrates, perhaps you need to move to find better food—jobs or people—in your life. If it waddles slowly like a duck from place to place, perhaps you need to stop rushing so much and be more aware of the present moment. The main point is to always ask an image what it is teaching you or leading you toward. Often your intuition or higher wisdom is being evoked.

I frequently see how the most skeptical and intellectual of people, when they are in the presence of birds and the wild, after a day or two come to see their resistances as paper walls and relax into feeling their kinship with other species. The animals are there. It is we who spend much conscious

---

63.   Paul Gruchhow, "Ancient Faith of Cranes," *Audubon Magazine* (New York: May 1989).

time removed from them. The more we pay attention, it seems the more we notice. When you are even more attuned, you find that animals come surprisingly close.

MORE OF GAIA'S TAPESTRY

In the foregoing chapters I have focused on some major wild animals that preoccupy us in dreams, thoughts, and art. Before leaving this Part, I want to zoom in on a few other fellow travelers and archetypes.

Just to keep things in perspective, we need to realize that we know how we humans classify animals but not how other animals sort us. To be sure, not by the size of our bank account or resume. Very likely they observe what is most present in us—degrees of aggression, anxiety, calmness or contentment.

People have objectified animals and sorted them out to help explain the world to themselves. They've been organized according to backbone (present or not), what is eaten (meat or vegetable), habitat (grassland, forest, tundra, alpine), mode of operation (two-legged, four-legged, winged). In all cases, classification must be seen as an intellectual construct overlaid onto the animal realm and subscribed to by general consensus. It's our attempt to fix the flux of vast animal variety and to be able to discuss it with a frame of reference. Doing so has been enormously helpful in regard to our attempts to analyze ecosystems in all their abundant detail. Species with names have a better chance at being saved than those without. But any artificial organization is subject to error. Moreover, we've only identified less than 10% of the species that actually live on Earth.

Classification has a human history. Aristotle, who died in 322 BC, presented his views in his *History of Animals* that endured for 2000 years. He posited that everything in Nature was made as it was for the sake of man (not woman). Everything had a Latin name and a genus but there was no sense of evolution or relation among species. Carl Linnaeus, the Swedish botanist, who lived from 1707–78, had the greatest influence until Darwin 100 years later. Like Aristotle, Linnaeus believed that the three kingdoms of nature (minerals, vegetables, and animals) were created for man by an omnipotent God. His innovation was to create a binomial system in which the old name for the genus was followed by its classification as species, which he saw as a group of organisms that were systematically related to each other. (Each creature in the animal world had a scientific name shared by no other). He then organized species into larger groups or genera, arranged analogous genera into Families, and related Families to Orders and Classes. He produced a strict hierarchy with the Kingdom at the apex.

But by the 19th century naturalists saw that this framework was too rigid to take into account the ever-increasing discoveries of fossil and living forms. When Charles Darwin and Alfred Russel Wallace came along, they described innumerable variations that occur in the progeny of nearly all living organisms. Darwin brought out how the struggle for existence ensures that the fittest survive and reproduce, so that variations are discarded or retained by natural selection; and how over time, these and other forces, such as reproductive isolation and sexual selection, led to the origin of new species. While man was still seen at the top by many, no longer could creatures be seen as created fully formed, but as the result of a slow process of transmutation.

The fundamentals of genetics were published by an Austrian monk (Gregor Mandel) in Darwin's time, but were ignored until Rosalind Franklin's x-ray diffraction photo of DNA in 1952 helped James Watson and Francis Crick solve the molecule's double-helix structure.[64] Now taxonomy is evolution-based, illustrating a history of the life forms that began once, perished or survived many mass extinctions, and changed innumerable times. Academics still hotly debate ancestorship and branching of kin in the tree of life. A major question is what forms will be most able to successfully survive, if we humans foul this biosphere.

Another way of organizing biodiversity that recent scientists have found useful is this hierarchy: ecosystem, community, guild, species, organism,

---

64. David Quammen, "Was Darwin Wrong?," National Geographic (Wash. D.C.: National Geographic Society, Nov. 2004), p. 32.

gene. For example, an animal lives in a certain ecosystem with a community of organisms that affect the food web and life cycle. The animal is a member of a guild, a set of species that live in the same place and harvest the same food similarly. It has genetic characteristics that link it to other organisms and species. Close analysis of ecosystems reveals the big and little players; their tightly bound inter-relationships help us know what they need to thrive.

Frogs

Long before the appearance of songbirds, the cries of frogs chorused from the melting of ice over the ponds to late summer. The Buddha-like frogs are extremely important to ecosystems, being the top carnivores of the detritus food chain (insects, worms), responsible for the decomposition of the forest floor. This chain recycles nutrients and minerals. Without this activity, trees would suffocate in their own waste. At the same time, amphibians are eaten by the carnivores of the grazing food chain (foxes, rabbits) and so are a link between the two chains, providing an essential energy and nutrient transfer.

Because frogs dwell in wetlands and have water-sensitive skin, they have taken the brunt of our environmental problems. Their thin skins absorb pollutants from both the soil and water, and since they don't migrate much, they suffer the problems of a particular region and reveal them to us. Acid rain, for instance, dissolved aluminum in soil and carried it into ponds that poisoned the creatures. High levels of ultraviolet light from ozone depletion have killed eggs of frogs that live at high altitudes in mountain forests. Frogs can't tolerate forest clearcuts because the toppling of trees removes shade from their spawning areas and exposes eggs to sunlight. Since the mid-1980's frog populations all over the world have declined so seriously that biologists warn about system collapse. Dozens of frog species qualify for protection under the Endangered Species Act but the U.S. Fish and Wildlife Service cannot keep up with the backlog nor do other research organizations receive enough funds to carry on studies.

While we have never liked seeing ourselves like frogs, many tales about them concern the pitfalls of ignoring them. Often a frog appears ugly until it is loved and then it turns into a prince. For instance, the Freudian psychoanalyst Bruno Bettelheim has commented on the story "The Frog King" (by Grimm), that the princess who at first ignores the frog must work out with him a mutual acceptance. In the end she married him in his prince aspect. In Freudian terms the frog would represent a young woman's fear, even abhorrence, of sexuality but that interpretation is far too limited. The frog that seems repulsive could be one's feelings of rage, shame, or revenge that one does not want to acknowledge. The stories teach how befriending or accepting them leads to positive transformation, the recovery of joy.

In the same way we could consider the plight of so many frogs perishing, give them mutual respect, and transform their situation on this Earth.

Turtles

Turtles, going their slow sure way, have stayed much the same since before the age of dinosaurs. Since the spread of humans, most turtles have suffered catastrophically.

Turtles of all sizes and shapes possess the secrets of the ages. Sea turtles bury their eggs in soil or sand to hide them from eaters. They also deposit nutrients that ecosystem watchers have noticed nourishes vegetation and stabilizes sand dunes. The mother turtles depend on the sun to incubate the eggs for several months, allowing for fluctuations of heat, moisture, and lateness of the season. Upon hatching, the turtles start at once to make their way to the water. They walk awkwardly but when they reach the wet sand bar and realize they are on the right track, they rush forward to the water, where they swim as gracefully as birds soar. Soon they are lost from view, and no one really knows where they go. The young are on their own, never to know their parents. The few that have been tracked show that they can live 140 years and be found 3000 miles away from where they were tagged. They are known to travel up to 1500 miles from nesting sites to very specific feeding areas. Turtles know no borders as they roam the Earth.

Their special qualities have made turtles central to stories about the creation of the world. Because the turtle is self-contained and stable, it was perceived as a cosmos unto itself, its hard back like the dome of heaven. It supported the world by the pillars of its four solid legs. For some Native American tribes before there was anything else there was a great turtle floating in a primal sea, and all the animals lived upon his carapace. Our continent was named Turtle Island by northwestern natives.

From childhood on, we learn how the turtle wins the race in the end because it is persistent, enduring, and focused.

The following dream shows a woman how to relate to the turtle:

> I am taking lessons from a man who is teaching a class on how to swim with sea turtles with your eyes open underwater. I am concerned that I will have a hard time handling this as I don't like to open my eyes under water. The turtles burrow under the sand in the water, and you have to watch the stirring of the sand to find out where they are; then you stand still, and they will come out. I try this and succeed in grabbing on to the turtle's shell as it comes out of the sand, and we swim like this through the crystal clear-water.

The dreamer is told that she must really go deep into the unconscious with her eyes open—that is, without trying to avoid any discomforts. Her ego-self has fears but perseveres. To reach the turtles she is told you have to be still and watchful. Then she experiences being carried along by a turtle as it glides through clear water, exhilarated by feeling the turtle's support and receiving fresh clarity.

The turtle is sacred because it is at home in water and on land, it carries splendid designs on its shell, and its heart beats on long after death. Its voice says to many men and women: Find a place in the sun. Don't be afraid of being alone. A few simpatico friends are all you need. Venture forth slowly but surely. Bask often in the warm free light.

Lions & Tigers

These big carnivores evolved in the once-abundant African savanna, living off the varieties of hoofed prey. They disappeared from our continent 10,000 years ago. Now all but extinct, they are primarily seen as rarities in zoos. Tiger parts have been traded and smuggled to supply a voracious Asian folk-medicine market. People consume tiger eyes to improve vision, tiger penises in soup to increase virility, crushed tiger bones to cure everything from acne to ulcers, tiger hearts and meat to bolster courage. In Asia, people consider the live animal a nuisance because it will attack them, but dead it is worth thousands of dollars. Those who traffic in animal parts value dollars, not their sacred majesty.

Lions and tigers show up frequently in imagery though as representations of physical prowess. In a typical example, Thomas Moore, author of *Care of the Soul*, reported that when he lay upon a massage table with two healers working on a particularly painful spot, "several large, brightly colored, imposing tigers leap out of a cage…They seemed at once playful and ferocious….The main things I felt from these tigers were courage, strength, and self-possession, qualities of heart I certainly needed at the time."[65]

In myths the Hindu Kali, goddess of creation and destruction rode a tiger and Shiva in his destruction aspect wore a tiger skin. Although archetypes of gods, interestingly, lions and tigers are not always brave and aggressive. Some are slackers and timid but members of a pride take care of them.

A dream of a <u>tiger with a bleeding paw</u> shows that a person's ability to move quickly and majestically has been cut. An action that will restore mobility and sense of mastery, such as acquiring a new skill or job, needs to be taken.

A woman dreams of having <u>a lion sit in her lap and petting it</u>. She did not feel afraid and so could be seen in good relation to her strong drive to ensure her survival against threats. This single woman 's life was strongly committed to a routine based on work and caring for her children. On the

---

65. Thomas Moore, *Care of the Soul* (New York: Harper Collins, 1992), pp. 160-1.

other hand, because of the size and strength of lions and tigers, their presence in thoughts or dreams could indicate an excessive amount of activity. A creative work may be consuming one; one may be in danger of workaholism. Establishing an equal partnership with this lion power is necessary.

Being thrown into a lion's den shows fear of being surrounded by attackers and the possibility of death. Jung had this dream at the time he was facing professional opposition by Freud, the founder of the Psychoanalytic Club. As he struggled with his intellectual differences from the establishment, he came to better realize his own contribution to the field of depth psychology. In a sense he experienced the death of an old bond and the beginning of a new path.

A woman with a doctorate in biology told how because of her love for wildlife, she pursued a science degree, which involved much data gathering in the field. She was consistently bothered by feeling that something was missing in this purely academic approach; nevertheless, she went to work for the Nature Conservancy, where she became even more frustrated with the lack of sympathy for any women's views. At this point she had her first dream of lions: I am looking for a spiritual retreat and climb high up on a rocky ridge. A male lion comes out of the bushes. I climb a fence to get away but the lion comes after me. Later that night she dreamed: A woman sits down beside me and becomes a lioness. I am told that the lioness was my teacher. She let these dreams sustain her in confronting her co-workers and not allowing herself and others to be ignored or abused.

Elephants

Elephants seem to be huge, ungainly creatures. Many people love them because in their presence they feel they can be themselves and not care what they look like. Elephants manifest exceptional qualities for which they have been revered, from time to time bedecked with flowers and praised for their beauty. From their lifestyle we can understand why.

Of all the animals considered so far, elephants belong to the tightest social groups, and these are structured by the females. A family unit consists of about 14 adult females and their offspring until they reach about 11 years. The oldest female is the leader, the matriarch, and in times of danger she fights. Males are forcibly ejected after about the age of 14 and roam around, mingling with other males.

Males in musth, with a hugely intensified testosterone level, become fierce and aggressive. Males mate better with age, the 50 year old bulls being the most successful of all. While females can mate with males at any time they are in estrus, they prefer and seek out a musth bull.

The grandiose powers of the females and musth males led to their being associated with gods. In India the elephant became a form of Shiva and his Goddess-spouse was Radha, known as "She-Elephant." Buddha was said to be the offspring of the virgin Maya and the elephant god under the name of Ganesha. The elephant-god was also worshipped in N. Africa and Egypt. In art, dreams, and visions elephants have frequently served as wise aids to humankind. They are the remover of obstacles, whether inner or outer. They safekeep the teachings of the ancients.

An important feature of elephants is their demonstrative caring and loyalty for one another. When one of their clan dies, the others come from far and wide to touch it all over, bury its carcass, carry off a bone. They greet one another excitedly by clicking tusks, reaching into each other's mouths with their trunks, flapping ears, spinning around, urinating, secreting from temporal glands between eye and ear, screaming, and trumpeting. They communicate with numerous calls, all of which are partly below the level of human hearing and carry for miles.

Elephants were used in armies in the Nile Valley in the time of pharaohs, by the Greeks, Carthaginians, Romans, Persians, and Asian kingdoms. They have also been exploited in plowing land and wood-harvesting, taught to lift and haul massive logs with their strong trunks.

While elephant species began about 40 million years ago, now only the African and Asian exist. Before humans hemmed them in parks, they migrated hundreds of miles seasonally and dominated the grassland ecology. In sufficient habitat they seek a new watering hole and feeding area every three weeks but they can quickly prune a small area of vegetation. With humans taking up more land, for instance in India, the clashes between people and elephants have escalated with deaths to both species.

As elephants age, so do the size of their tusks. These tusks, which have a lustrous diamond-shaped core, have been relentlessly and illegally pursued by traffickers to supply the ivory market. In the wild, elephants easily live 50 or 60 years but now few reach even 35 so no elders are around to pass along elephant culture. The problem with killing off the older ones is that it is they who have lived through many crises and explored much terrain and can pass on this knowledge to the new generations.

So when we reflect upon or dream about elephants today, one of the messages is that of an impoverished society that has lost the wisdom of its elders.

A man has presented a proposal, on which he and his team have worked several months, to the decision-makers of the company. They are not interested. He walks away, lonely and sad. An elephant nuzzles him with its trunk. He thinks he is blind because he can't see too well. He is afraid of touching the animal but he reaches out and caresses it. It is fearful about the future, starving and unable to support itself.

The man's future, like the elephant's, is uncertain. Both have been defeated, both coping with loss of sustenance. In this dream the man realizes his bond with the elephant. Another man might not have been able to reach out to the elephant as this man does. This man's vision is clouded, meaning that he is not seeing the situation clearly, but he does reach out in trust. He has a big ally. The elephant's size and wisdom are factors, suggesting the man contains a lot more than he realizes. The elephant also needs the man's help to keep from dying.

Monkeys and the Big Apes

The current picture of the Hominid family tree—including us—shares 96.4% DNA structure. Fifteen million years ago orangutans branched off, nine million years ago gorillas. The upright hominids, including *Australopitheccus, Homo habilis, Homo erectus, Homo sapiens* started six million years ago. We share with chimps a more recent ancestor that the gorilla does not share, from whom we both branched only five million years ago, a blink in evolutionary time. Although we did not evolve directly from chimps, we are 98.4% identical, prompting physiologist and ecologist Jared Diamond to classify us as a third species of chimps. Genetic grouping shows ape and humans more closely related than African elephants and Indian elephants. Current chimps have stayed closer to our common ape ancestor. The innovations appearing in humans—our features as bipedal, big-brained, and highly vocal—are contained in chimp anatomy, and started far earlier in the primate line than either of us. Our brain is twice the size of chimps but a genetic program that would allow brain cells in a chimp fetus to go through one more doubling would make up the difference. The human face is tucked under the brain case instead of projecting beyond as in a chimp.

Most primates can be seen in zoos rather than the wild, which is a pity because they look so much better in their natural habitat, where they're supposed to be. Imagine studying human primates kept in prison cells: how much good-spirited behavior would you observe?

Some monkeys, such as the macaques (including rhesus and langur varieties), are very numerous, while the apes (chimpanzee, gorilla, orangutan) are quite endangered due to loss of forest habitat. In the Brazilian jungle, home of the last 400 golden lion tamarins, only a bit of the original rainforest is left. Poachers steal these creatures and sell them for $20,000 or more apiece. With so few left, one virus could wipe out the entire population. Left alone, primates are easy on a habitat because they are largely vegetarian and forage lightly, eating part of a plant here and there, giving it time to regenerate.

In reflecting on primates, the distinctions among them are worth noticing. For instance, capuchins are very small, gorillas very large, spider monkeys very acrobatic. The tails of monkeys are a special feature; these serve as a fifth hand, enabling monkeys to take flying leaps across branches with great speed. Apes have no tail but more mental skills, such as the ability to learn words and sign language from humans, which are, interestingly, not skills they would use in their natural surroundings. Primate families stay together, communicating with a variety of meaningful sounds that we have termed belches, grunts, barks, cries, screams, growls, and roars. Enjoying play, they somersault, swing, slide, giggle, and play tricks, all the while making expressive faces. They are not shy about their genitals, examining them in detail. The vivid invitation of the baboon's magenta hindquarters may make us blush. They eat with gusto, smacking their lips. They spend hours grooming one another to strengthen their bonds. They express themselves more blatantly than we do—from being upset to showing off—with less conscious denial.

Primates show a need for acceptance in groups, as we do. They give to one another, trusting that the favor will be returned. Those who do not give back are shunned, as we do to one another. Conflicts are worked out in numerous ways: holding hands, kissing, defending one another, uttering certain sounds.

Violence among the big apes is of special interest to us humans because of our kinship. Dian Fossey, who researched gorillas, said that she would observe only about five minutes of violence to every 3000 hours.[66] Studies of some chimps document rape, border raids, brutal beatings and warfare among rival territorial gangs, acts of lethal aggression that we observe in humans too. Consider the wars, tortures, and terrorism we conduct on our own kind. We do other animals wrong by projecting aggression onto them solely. People tend to accept the genetic connection for attachment, cooperation, and sex but not aggression, despite daily evidence on television broadcasts of human brutality.

Primates also display consistent kindness and empathy, developing these traits in the same way humans do. An example of compassion that made the newspapers was the gorilla who scooped up and carried to safety the three year old boy who had fallen 18 ft. into the primate exhibit at the Chicago Brookfield Zoo.[67] A pygmy chimp, the bonobo, is known as one

---

66.   Dian Fossey, *Gorillas in the Mist* (Boston, MA: Houghton-Miflin, 1983).

67.   Frans B. M. de Waal, "Survival of the Kindest," (*New York Times,* August 22, 1996), OP-ED.

of the most peaceful, unaggressive mammals alive. Notably they don't eat meat or fight for status. Quick, casual sexual strokes are given to each other—to male and female, young and old alike—in order to appease the social order.

Traditional scientists have a tough time acknowledging that animals act unselfishly. But some are breaking ranks, recognizing that truth is not being served by such a narrow view. Primatologist, Frans de Waal, author of *Good Natured: The Origins of Right and Wrong in Humans and Other Animals*, points out that if scientists say animals cheat, then they should also say that they can be honest; if they make enemies, they make friends; if they call them spiteful, they should also be acknowledged as empathetic.

However, there is still a vested interest among scientists to put distance between humans and other primates. Doing so makes it easier for primates to be used for medical, food, and cosmetic research without ethical considerations. Monkeys, especially rhesus (because of the Rh factor in human blood), are captured by the thousands for manipulation in laboratories. Because apes are genetically close to us, their parts can be used for transplants. Jane Goodall, who has devoted her life to rescuing chimps and educating the public about them, deplores how our closest relatives are deliberately infected with AIDS, kept in cages, fitted with electric collars, having their feet bound, teeth pulled and otherwise cruelly treated. Dreams that contain images of maltreated primates show that we treat ourselves as violently as we may treat others. The same can be said of compassion.

Monkeys have important literary and religious positions. The most popular book of Chinese history, called *Journey to the West*, written in the 1500's, featured Monkey as a priest who battles for enlightenment. Mao Tse Tung liked to compare himself to "Monkey." In India the hanuman, a species of langurs, is sacred. The god Hanuman was son of the wind and a monkey nymph. Since he helped the deity Rama (the seventh avatar of Vishnu), hanumans have been protected and most often seen in the company of holy men. Temples and shrines are dedicated to the monkey god Hanuman. Like humans, he is often excessive, comic, destructive, forgetful, and lively. He is very popular now because people see in this image a link between God, animal and human, an image of a power that can leap over obstacles.

Skunks

Everyone knows that skunks venture forth mostly at night and get killed by cars often. It is probably less appreciated how helpful skunks are to farmers in that they eat great quantities of annoying mice, rats, and insects.

People who have been too nice often have skunk dreams. A self-effacing woman dreamed of <u>giving birth to a skunk born in manure</u>. This means that in the pile of shit a rebellious spirit is born. Time to stop putting up with smoldering resentment and blast one or two others. "To skunk someone" in sports means to beat them soundly. You show them what's what, no doubt about it. The same person later dreamed that <u>learning how to feed skunks was important</u>. Being self-protective, like skunks, and capable of repelling annoyances are vital life skills.

Squirrels, Rats & Mice

These rodents gnaw. Gnawers have large incisors that grow constantly so they do not get worn down. Ecologically rodents are of value because they keep forest grasses trimmed and their digging and burrowing helps make soil fertile. Every nut a squirrel buries is a potential tree. Most oak, hickory, and walnut trees around today exist because of squirrels' industry. They also serve as food for about 160 species, including snakes, hawks, owls, foxes, and raccoons.

Gnawing animals appear in your psyche when something is bothering you and disturbing your peace. That something, when pursued, leads you to necessary forms of action.

Stephen Gallegos, the therapist who focuses primarily on animal imagery in therapy, described an experience he had. Despite his extensive work with other people, he felt "socially retarded." Lying on his bed, he asked his psyche if there was an animal of social injury that he should meet with.

> Immediately a squirrel appears, but he has a crutch and his left rear leg is heavily bandaged. I am aware of how cumbersomely he gets around, whereas squirrels usually scurry quite rapidly. I ask him what he needs from me and he tells me that I need to unbandage his leg. I do as he asks and he then tells me that I need to touch the wound. It is an open wound, very raw; there is no skin on most of his leg. I put my hand on the warm muscle that is exposed and feel both his sensitivity and my own tendency to withdraw from that contact. As I leave my hand on his wounded leg I have fleeting memories of myself as a child. My father is teaching me how to be social, rigidly instructing me that when I meet someone I am to shake hands with them, greet them, and tell them my name. Then I am to say nothing more until I am spoken to. I am aware of my own discomfort and of his rigidity, remembering that he only went as far as third grade in school. The squirrel then throws away his crutch and begins to scurry around much more easily, but his left leg is still bent. He is happy that he no longer has to use the crutch and that the heavy bandage is gone. So even though he is not as quick as the other squirrels, he is much more skillful at getting around than he was before. I thank him.

After that he was able to feel much more at ease and at home with people, comfortable for the first time in his life.

A quite different energy emanates from rats. Originating in Asia, these great emigrants have followed humans by foot, in carts, ships, trains, and trucks. These survivors eat everything we eat, plus paint, soap, leather, garbage, sewage, and even corpses. Those who live in filthy areas become degraded (just as humans do) but those who live in clean conditions are as clean as squirrels. However, they have been blamed for spreading diseases that have killed more humans than all wars and revolutions put together.

Rats are intelligent, quick to learn and remember, and prolific—qualities that humans exploit in laboratories. A female bears 15–16 litters of eight babies a year. The babies are born 21 days after conception. The female breeds again within a few hours or week. At three weeks the young ones are ready to go off on their own, and at three months are ready to breed. They can keep this breeding up for two years and die out by their third year.

Subconsciously, our deepest desires eat away at us. Sometimes we hate to do anything about them, being scared and nauseous about the steps required. An aggressive inner rat will torture you and spoil things until you take action.

Here's a dream that conveys the gnawing pain a child felt when his mother and father were too busy to notice him. <u>I am left in a bare room with a plate on which is a dead rat covered with oil. I plead and argue against having to eat this rat.</u> The dreamer remembered how horrible it felt to have to accept the pain of his parents' absence; he had no recourse, except to eat it, which his psyche presents as a dead rat. The adult can handle the message of this dream by acknowledging the emotional gravity of being without love. Doing so gives renewed vigor. As a child, the pain is absorbed, but not articulated.

Loren Eiseley tells how having a visitation by a live rat can seem like a "personal message from the dark." In *The Night Country* he described an incident that seemed 'intellectual' in quality. He was at a gathering where a famous novelist held forth on how it was just a matter of time before "man would turn the whole earth into a garden of Eden for his own enjoyment." Unnoticed by anyone else except Eiseley, a rat reared up under the man's chair as if in contempt.[68]

Scientists analyzing the mouse genome have found that humans and mice contain 99% of the same genes, although humans contain 14% more DNA in total.[69] This factor gives scientists even greater incentive to use mice as surrogates for humans in finding the genetic roots of disease. Mice evolved by living close to us. Because they eat what we do and enjoy our homes as their habitats, their populations exploded worldwide. This case of mice shows how "nature" lives inside our homes, not just "out there."

---

68. Loren Eiseley, *The Night Country* (New York: Scribner's, 1971), pp. 33-5.

69. Nicholas Wade, "Comparing Mouse Genes to Man's and Finding a World of Similarity" (*New York Times*, December 5, 2002).

*   *   *

This romp amidst wild animals can lead you to insights about your inner self and participation in the outer world. The foregoing chapters show how animal behavior teaches us to look beneath surface appearances, to trust our intuition more, to face the darkness, to challenge predators inside and out, to become sharp, wily and shrewd. With animal ferocity, we can learn to attack cruelties of our culture and not suppress our deeper feelings. We can turn our wits into sharp claws and teeth. Animals show us how to endure and how to die with dignity (without fanfare and with quiet humility).

Gaia offers so many animals to muse upon. One of the best ways to strengthen your connection with them is to imagine that you are an animal, letting its being infuse you for a time. In the dancer/healer Anna Halprin's workshops, she asks people to draw a self-portrait, then spend a half-hour acting as a chosen animal in its habitat, followed up by drawing a self-portrait again. The second one is strikingly bolder and darker.

A woman with cancer used her animal to attack her malignancy. She crouched on the floor like an alligator, feeling her face change and extend into a snout, sensing her spine lengthen and stiffen. She growled and leaped, tearing at her victim's clothes and then dragging it out of the room. She felt that this experience gave her a taste of power beyond herself to conquer her disease.

Another approach is to get into a meditative state and call a council meeting of the animals who are important to you. On the agenda put your needs and theirs. Letting a dialogue take place is one of the techniques described for working with animals in the last chapter.

PART TWO: Domesticated Animals

PREFACE

Appearing much more recently in the branching tree of life, domestic animals are vastly different from wild animals.

These animals were so controlled by humans that they became dependent, unable to survive without us. Wild animals are still more or less independent, despite our increasing attempts to "manage" them. Tigers and dolphins can be taught tricks, elephants can be made to pull plows, but they remain frustrated slaves, never content. If we hold birds captive, they bond with us and, if set free, suffer tragic consequences. Domesticated animals gave up their wild spirit long ago.

Once upon a time humans too could have been called "wild," as they hunted other animals for food, scratched for roots, ate leaves, and lived in caves. They had the foresight to be thrifty with their prey, using bones for tools, skin and hair for clothes and blankets, and various parts for medicine and jewelry. Now few of us know any more what to do in wild country than the animals we've subdued. This major distinction between the wild and domestic is reflected in our psyches too. Hence, the division of this book into two parts—the wild and the domesticated.

In this section on domestic animals, I'll review farm animals first. Then horses, who fall somewhere between farm animals and household pets. Lastly, household cats and dogs.

Domestication, which turned out to be revolutionary, occurred when early peoples realized that to offset shortages in wild game, grain, nuts and fruit, they could set about growing their own. Thus, instead of being hunters and foragers, they became farmers. According to *The Cambridge Encyclopedia of Human Evolution,* here is the order in which common domestic animals were adapted.

ANIMAL	WILD PROGENITOR	PRINCIPAL REGION OF ORIGIN	APPROXIMATE DATE OF DOMESTICATION
Dog	Wolf	Western Asia	12,000 years ago
Pig	Boar	Turkey	10,400-10,000 " "
Goat	Bezoar goat	Western Asia	9,000 " "
Sheep	Asiatic mouflon	Western Asia	9,000 " "
Cattle	Aurochs	Western Asia	8,000 " "
Horse	Horse	Central Asia	6,000 " "
Cat	Cat	Western Asia	5,000 " "?
Chicken	Jungle fowl	Southern Asia	4,000 " "

As the centuries passed, to a large extent the history of domestication became synonymous with the history of genetic engineering, the continuous modification of animals for our own purposes. Breeders have long created forms with altered temperaments, size, strength, appearance, fertility, milk, meat and egg production. Desired types are kept; the others destroyed. In the process animals have lost the alertness, sensitivity, and wiles that living in the wild engenders. They have been reduced both in intelligence and resistance to disease.

Considering the whole world as our consulting room, it's crucial that we examine our relationship with them. As with family members, close contact has enabled some of us to become more familiar with the ways of these animals as well as to take them more for granted. So in a strange way we have become both more aware and less aware of them. In our psyches they are closer to consciousness and reveal themselves more easily to us than wild ones because of their accessibility. But failing to treat them ethically exposes a dysfunctional side of ourselves.

At present our treatment of domesticated animals appears to fluctuate between exploitation and nurturance. The shaping of our future selves and world will be strongly influenced by how we resolve this conflict in our hearts. So much depends on whether we grow more warm and caring or cold and detached.

ON THE FARM: PIGS, CATTLE, SHEEP, CHICKENS, GOATS

In early days and wherever family farms persist, animals are considered part of the household. The cost of feeding them is budgeted into the family finances. The animals are given dwelling areas. In exchange, they are expected to work or provide a service.

In some villages around the world, farm animals still live quite close to the family members, even under the same roof. In Costa Rica, for instance, people use the top floor for themselves and the bottom floor for the horses, sheep, and cows. In Europe walled-in family compounds include not only the house for the family but also quarters for the animals. With such close ties, people naturally have had mixed feelings toward the animals they raise for the marketplace. Farm animals have been pampered, beaten, sexually used, and honored for their gifts.

As societies became more industrialized, people hung around their farm animals less and the emotional gulf between them widened. Use of the term "livestock" enabled people to move from the specific to the abstract in their regard for the animals. ("Cattle" came from the combination of the legal words "chattel" and "capital"). As family farms were supplanted by the factory farming practices of large corporations, animals were considered little more than biological meat machines. Hate is said to be the opposite of love, but indifference is the absence of either emotion.

We mustn't forget that our embryos share features with farm animals, as photographs have documented. In them one sees how the embryos of a chicken at two days, a pig at 21 days, and a human at 31 look very similar. As a human embryo develops, what could have been a snout (for a pig) will become a nose. A human fetus practices feeding by reflexively sucking its thumb, just as a chick practices pecking. The chick's "thumb" is derived from the same ancestral form as a human index finger. All vertebrates' limbs start looking like fin-buds. As they lengthen, cartilage coalesces into five digits. For the making of a pig, the fifth digit disappears; in a chicken, the fifth digit becomes a vestigial spur. The differences between us and other vertebrates are more of a degree than of kind. This shared ancestry is most visible before birth, before further development in all its variations takes over.[70]

Animals on the Pre-Industrial Farm

Life for farm animals is conditioned by how humans raise them. The practices and rhythms of family farms have been handed down over the generations. One such farmer says: "(Farmers and ranchers) love their animals and have a great respect for them. If they didn't, they wouldn't sacrifice so much for their care. It's not a nine to five, weekends off (job), it's 24/seven, and the animals get taken care of first every day, and there's no calling in sick."

While small farms—those with gross sales of less than $20,000—still comprise 2/3 of U.S. total of "farms", they account for just 4% of the nation's agricultural sales. The average age of the "small" farmer is 58; his or her children have gone to work in the cities. He or she probably has other part-time employment. Yet there is a fierce attachment to this difficult way of life. These farmers feel they have a noble purpose in "feeding the people."[71]

On small farms the scent of freshly mown hay mingles with the acrid odor of urine-soaked and decomposing dung piles. Throughout the day may be heard the muffled chorus of fowl, an occasional low, sustained moo, and chomping and grunting from the pig pens. The feathers of chickens range from burnished copper to black and white designs.

---

70. Embryonic images by scientific photographer, Lennart Nilsson, as seen in *Life Magazine* (New York: Nov. 1996).

71. *Bozeman Chronicle* (Montana, Sept. 15, 1996).

Something about barns draws us, makes us feel at ease, glad to be away from the pretensions of our own kind.

The animals have distinct life cycles, as well as their ways of eating, resting, mating, nursing their young, and dying but for commercial reasons, these life cycles have been increasingly interfered with. Here's a quick roundup of primary farm animals.

PIGS

Pigs, bred from wild boars, were the earliest creatures to be adapted for domestication. They required little labor since they could be left to forage with their upturned snouts for roots and grubs throughout the settlement. In doing so, the pigs helped cultivate the soil. They also made efficient use of their food energy, converting 35% into meat, compared with 13% for sheep or 6.5% for cattle. These short-legged, round-bellied, floppy-eared animals with sensitive skins and curlicued tails proved themselves to be smarter than dogs and affectionate. In some countries, such as Ecuador, people lead pigs around on leashes and take them on buses.

In Papua New Guinea, the pigs are wiry, bristly and dark; not naked and pink like many of ours. They represent wealth and social standing. While sometimes used as barter, there is no attempt to raise them as a commodity. Women take care of them, love and pet them, scratch and de-tick them, even sleep with them. Women will even suckle the pigs, behavior that is denounced by missionaries.

SHEEP

Although descended from smart wild ancestors, domestic sheep have been bred so that they've become the meekest of animals, harmless, and naive. They are very vulnerable to predators, as well as parasites, skin infections and other diseases. In the spring when lambs are born, the lambs stay with their mother for the summer. Then their owners decide whether they are to be sold for slaughter or allowed to mature and breed more lambs. Aside from their meat, their wool is the basis for our finest fabrics.

The predominant rule of the range is to kill any animal that harms or interferes with a farmer's possessions. Yet, there exists a minority group of sheep farmers who use llamas to protect the flocks and don't shoot wolves or coyotes. Such farmers can market their products under the name of "Predator Friendly," a label that increases the prices but appeals to customers who prefer this approach.

GOATS

Goats like companionship and fun, will jump and caper. They are hardy, intelligent, and precocious. Also quite fastidious, they are unwilling to eat hay off the floor.

The rutting males emit a strong odor from behind their horns and can breed a lot of females quickly. Kids are born after a 150-day gestation period and can soon stand. They are taken from their mothers so that humans can collect the milk from the does. Goats can live 12 years.

People have long used their milk (from which they also make cheese), their meat, their hide, and their hair (for example, the quite special mohair). In the old days a man's wealth was determined by how many goats; herds multiplied into the billions. Goats exist in more countries than other farm animals because they can survive anywhere, even climb onto crevices of mountain ranges and trees.

This ability made them more responsible for stripping land of vegetation far more than mining. Goats are primary causes in the making of the Sahara Desert and ecologically impoverished land in Greece and the Middle East. "The mark of the goat is upon our planet perhaps forever," Roger Caras wrote in *A Perfect Harmony*.[72]

CHICKENS

A chick emerges from an egg after 21 days. Free range chickens like to peck quietly for leaves, roots, bulbs, and seeds with their sharp beaks and scratching claws under the watchful eyes of their roosters. They have small wings that enable them to glide in short flights only. Chickens establish a "pecking order," by conducting a sort of tournament between pairs. (We do likewise, if not in the workplace, then in our minds).

---

72.   Roger Caras, *A Perfect Harmony* (New York: Simon & Schuster, 1996), p. 52.

Because putting roosters into each other's territory activates their territorial fighting spirit, inducing cockfights was done by the Romans, Greeks, Egyptians, Persians, and so on throughout the centuries. Cockfights were used to inspire courage and bloodlust in soldiers. Now while legal statutes outlaw cockfighting in most of our states, officials generally let this underground enterprise flourish.

To see if cocks would make good fighters, they may be punctured with an ice pick to see if they will fight back. If cocks pass such a test, they are subjected to training for weeks of running back and forth along a 4-foot-long training table to strengthen their legs and being tossed into air in order to strengthen their wings. Their muscles are massaged. With spurs covered, they are thrown into practice matches with each other.

In the arena where fights take place, the cocks are paraded so people can make bets. The birds are dropped into a "pit". After the birds are released, they peck and jab until one is dead or forfeits. If a bird refuses to fight, he is usually killed by his owner anyway. After a tournament piles of dead birds are torn to shreds. If this repels you, it is nothing compared to the brutality of factory farming.

CATTLE

A typical sight in the land of open sky and rolling hills is cattle moving slowly as they eat, perhaps lounging while chewing their cud, or standing on river banks with forelegs in the water.

Cattle can weigh up to 3000 lbs. They can drink 40 gallons of water on a hot day, putting a huge demand on water supplies. With no front teeth on their upper jaws, they graze by wrapping their tongues around the plants and pulling.

Calves are born in late winter and early spring. In severe weather they are likely to freeze to death. A mother licks her baby off, bonding with it, and moos. The calf, standing soon after birth, recognizes its mother's particular sound.

Dairy calves are taken away from their mothers after one or two days so humans get the mothers' milk. Calves designed for beef stay with their mothers on the range. At two-three months they are brought in for branding and given shots. Males, not destined for breeding, are castrated. At six months the calves are separated from their mothers for a month, then put back together again and expected to be independent. Steers are sold for meat when they reach 1000 lbs.

Steers bred for beef usually have shorter legs than dairy cows, long straight backs, sturdy bodies. It is estimated that each needs to feed on about 40 acres of land. In an effort to circumvent the cost of roughage, farmers have been known to feed them cardboard or force plastic pot scrubbers wrapped in masking tape down their throats. The steers' need to taste, smell, and to ruminate is thus disregarded.

By contrast, in some cultures, such as India and Mexico, the animals are bedecked with ribbons and flowers and paraded to the accompaniment of music. Priests bless them in gratitude for all the nourishing gifts they have provided and will continue to do so.

When you talk to those who have grown up on farms, you occasionally hear of favorite animals. Even children, whose first response is curiosity rather than cruelty, learn before long that they cannot get attached to a calf, goat, or lamb because it will have to be slaughtered soon. As feelings for the animals are suppressed, so is sensitivity to their needs. Children learn not to name the animals and to take pride in winning cash prizes in 4-H contests. But the practices of factory farming distance us from the animals even more radically.

An Assemblage of Parts

Industrial farms owned by large corporations treat animals solely as commodities, not creatures whose inner organs are as tender as their own. Making efficiency and yield top priorities, people engineered the storage, transportation, and processing of animal foods that turned the livestock business into a multi-billion dollar industry. It should be alarming that this industry is in the hands of relatively few corporations. Four meat packers control 90% of meat processing. Some 2% of all private corporations monopolize 90% of the cattle, hog, and poultry industries. The top U.S. agribusinesses are: Philip Morris, Cargill, Pepsico, Coca-Cola, ConAgra,

RJR Nabisco, Anheuser Busch. And, closely allied with the petrochemical-food corporations are the biomedical-pharmaceutical companies.

It's also deeply ironic that while our debt to domestic animals for their food products and hides is incalculable and entire industries are formed because of them, the animals themselves are treated in appalling ways. Perhaps if we took the trouble to visit processing establishments, we'd have massive protests. Those of us who do like meat don't want to get near them, likely knowing we'd be revolted if we did. It's enough to buy the packaged food in supermarkets and not think about what came before. No longer do we see the chicken, lamb or cow we eat. We are largely unconscious of where our meat comes from. This needs to be changed.

We also have to ask what happens to the psyches of the people working in these places? Whenever individuals conduct mass slaughters, they are known to become morose, taciturn, and heavy consumers of alcohol. They "are doing their job" but hardening themselves to the animals' pain. Many workers evade responsibility for actions that their gut tells them is wrong by saying they just carry out orders. A slaughterhouse human-resources director says he has the hardest time to get people to work and many have repetitive injuries ("There are times when the ambulance comes several times a day. It's awful."[73]) Some people are strong enough not to sacrifice their feelings for current job conditions and others are not.

Here's a quick survey of the life dished out to pigs, chickens, and cows on factory farms. Sheep and goats are not so affected by such practices.

First pigs. Instead of giving pigs free range, employees confine them for their entire lives in giant buildings, where they must stand on concrete grates that allow their wastes to drop into giant vats below. Employees flush the wastes, creating a slurry that increases its volume but makes it easier to manage. The slurry is dumped in tanks, which can crack when it rains. Spills happen regularly, as in N. Carolina where 25 million gallons recently spilled and killed a 17-mile stretch of river. These wastes are also dispersed over land, where they run into rivers and contaminate the ground water. The fumes cause respiratory diseases in a majority of the humans and pigs in the vicinity. Because the unbearable odor,

---

73. Eric Weddle, *The New Yorker* (New York: April 24 & May 1, 2000), p. 146.

monumental pollution, and plague of flies generate hostility among neighbors, corporate owners keep searching for areas where they can find less people and regulations.

Sows are artificially inseminated, their piglets weaned early. Because young pigs bite each others' tails in these cramped, barren environments, employees cut off their tails. The pigs are given numerous injections but no pain relievers. A technician writes: "The breeding sow should be thought of, and treated as, a piece of machinery whose function is to pump out baby pigs like a sausage machine."[74]

In the chicken industry the animals are divided according to function in dark, fecal dust-filled warehouses. Egg-laying females have beaks removed to keep them from pecking each other in their tightly packed wire cages. Sometimes the hens' feet just grow around the wire at the bottom. A chicken's natural life is 15 or more years, but in egg factories the average lifespan is two years. Broilers are kept so they can't move and develop muscles. They are allowed to live for two months.

In an article about a Tyson plant, the New York Times reported:

> Modern processing plants are a far cry from grabbing a chicken by the neck and whacking off its head. Live chickens empty onto a conveyor belt that leads to a darkened room, where workers hang them upside down from U-shaped shackles on an assembly line. The birds are stunned with an electric shock, their throats slit by machine and they move through boiling water to loosen the feathers. Machines massage off the feathers, eviscerate and wash the birds inside and out, and slice them into pieces.[75]

After slaughtering and processed for breading, cooking and freezing operations, the remaining feathers, heads, blood and internal organs are collected and sent to a rendering plant to become ingredients in chicken

---

74. Humane Farming Association.

75. Douglas Frantz, "How Tyson Became the Chicken King," *New York Times* (August 28, 1994).

and cattle feed and pet food. Chicken feet, called paws, are shipped to China for use in soups and appetizers.

On to the cattle industry. In order to be cost effective, factory farmers often treat their cattle in the same manner as pigs with confinement and continuous doses of antibiotics and other drugs. We've long known that to produce veal, calves are denied all solid food. In order to keep their meat tender, calves are kept from moving and are forced to lie in their own excrement. They become anemic and have chronic diarrhea. Many dairy cows are injected with a genetically engineered hormone called recombinant Bovine Growth Hormone, a suspected carcinogen in humans and a cause of stress in the cows. This is administered to increase the cows' milk production, even though every year farmers are forced out of business because production outreaches demand. (In 1985 alone, the government paid over 14,000 dairy farmers to kill cows and get out of the business. 1.62 million cows were killed or exported.)

The pressure to increase production is a primary cause of forest destruction throughout the world. For every quarter pound of hamburger exported from S. America by McDonalds, Burger King, or the other chains, 55 square feet of rain forest is destroyed along with 165 pounds of unique life forms. The methane produced by flatulence is also a major contributor to global warming.

People at an efficient slaughterhouse process 250 cows an hour, 16 hours a day, breaking them into dozens of parts as the carcasses flow down the line on steel hooks. The blood is collected and later baked for use in a protein-rich animal feed. The hooves are removed, the hide stripped for sale as leather and suede. The head is sliced off, the chest opened, and the internal organs removed. The carcass yields about 568 pounds of beef and 49 pounds of organs and glands. The fat and bones are used for many things: floor wax, cosmetics, candles, pet food. Horns are used for gelatin and collagen. Medicines are also derived.

To the credit of the industry, stockowners have welcomed the ideas of a woman, who has made the inevitable killing of cattle less tortuous. She is an animal scientist named Dr. Temple Grandin, whose autism enabled her to empathize with the cows' plight. Taking a cue from her problems with a nervous system dominated by fear and the urge to flee, like her subjects, she remedied the handling procedures that frightened cows. "We've got to get rid of the cowboy rodeo stuff, the yelling and screaming at them, forcing them," she said. Looking at feedlots and ramps from the cows' perspective, she determined that distractions, such as Styrofoam cups, chains jingling, shadows, a coat on a fence, or seeing a person through slats, had to be eliminated. She pointed out that cows don't like to enter closed spaces but will not balk at curved chutes. Non-slip footing, no sharp edges, prods with plastic ribbons were other ideas that made the process easier. So is a device that holds them on the sides, close to the animal in front, with gentle pressure and guidance to the holding area for the kill. Today because of her efforts, most cattle in the U.S. and Canada are managed in facilities she designed.[76]

Dr. Grandin, who has devoted her work to making life less painful for cattle, sees them as living, feeling creatures, not machines. She is an outstanding example of how one person can bring compassion to a large-scale industry. Other influential people are those who give their farm animals outdoor ranges, grass and sunlight.[77]

When we recognize that we have a personal relationship with the world we live in, we have to pay attention to the warning signs that result from neglect, ignorance, or deliberate profit-seeking,. Among our most prominent concerns are health issues and biotechnology. One cause of the outbreaks of salmonella and E.coli attacks is that to save money industrial farmers often add waste substances to livestock and poultry feed, as has been described. Mad cow disease (formally known as bovine spongiform encephalopathy) has been linked to fatal brain disease in humans with an incubation period of 10–40 years. The disease is believed to come from the practice of feeding cattle ground up offal of sheep (not allowed in the U.S.). Furthermore, the toxins in animals' intestines spill in slaughterhouses and make their way into food. The *New England Journal of Medicine*, U.S. Centers for Disease Control, Natural Resources Defense

---

76. Temple Grandin, "Qualities of an Animal Scientist," *New York Times* (August 5, 1997), p. B9.

77. For locations of where you can buy meat from such farms, see www.eatwild.com.

Council, and U.S. Food and Drug Administration all warn that levels of antibiotics and other contaminants pose serious threats to the health of consumers. It is also being studied how the stress and fear of the animals slaughtered affect the behavior and metabolism of us consumers.

And not least, the most invested-in industry at present—biotechnology, the manipulation of genes to our purposes—has all sorts of implications, positive and negative. In 1997 the news broke that Scotland researchers cloned the first lamb. Dr. Ian Wilmut (of the Scotland cloning group) says his aim is "to turn animals into factories churning out proteins that can be used as drugs."[78] Less than six months later 10 cows in Wisconsin were cloned by the same method. Human cloning is no longer waiting in the wings but moving onto center stage.

Genetic tinkering is the ultimate in viewing living creatures as a mechanism of organs, tissues, cells, and other parts. Absent is the seeing of the animal existing for its own sake and in relation to others. No doubt many of us feel wary of how biological structures will infiltrate our bodies and lives. We have to dig deeper and see how unconsciously we are playing God, as the myths of old show us repeatedly that the seizing of too much power leads to punishing destruction. (The atom bomb is a modern example.)

It is also too easy for those who treat animals as objects to disregard their "rights" altogether. Farm animals are explicitly excluded from the Animal Welfare Act because they are considered the "property" of their owners. Laws give more protection to animals in kennels, stables, laboratories, and zoos. In zoos, for instance, the practices of long-term confinement, castration, and no anesthetic are not acceptable, but they are allowed for farmers because to attend to these measures would increase their costs and be time-consuming. Polls indicate that the majority of the general public, except farmers, believe animal production systems should be regulated with respect to animal welfare. One ethical question to resolve is whether farm animals "belong" to the consuming public (via agencies like the USDA) or to the farmer? Whose views should prevail in this mess?

---

78. Michael Specter with Gina Kolata, "After Decades and Many Missteps, Cloning Success," *New York Times* (March 3, 1997), p.1.

In a pertinent poem, called "Animals and People, The Human Heart in Conflict with Itself," Pattiann Rogers asks:

> For how can we possess dignity
> if we allow them no dignity? Who will recognize our beauty
> if we do not revel in their beauty? How can we hope
> to receive honor if we give no honor? How can we believe
> in grace if we cannot bestow grace?

DREAMS & VISIONS OF BARNYARD ANIMALS

Our dreams and visions attempt to restore us to sanity. Dreams of <u>cows in crowded stalls, agitated stamping or lying on the plain, panting, near death</u> reflect the crowded conditions of cattle in factory farms. They want out, just as something in us wants to escape that confinement, that death march.

Since many of us live in cities, rural values have been lost. Many people feel nostalgic, regretful about adapting to a high technology, super-fast, insulated way of life instead of being outdoors and engaged in meaningful work. Farm animals in our memories, dreams, and reflections remind them that happiness and fulfillment are to be found in renewing respect for the land, allowing it and its inhabitants time to regenerate and be fertile, of maintaining the purity of water and its fish, of feeling rooted to a place, and caring for it.

Even the ubiquitous manure pile, found on all farms, is a source of positive meaning, both literally and figuratively. Excrement may smell bad and repel but it is organic matter that biological activity will convert into new life. The manure pile—the end waste pile—is also the new beginning pile. We like to call our resentments, angers, boredom, inanities the "pile of shit." Or, we say, "getting our shit together," meaning all the ragged emotions we don't bother to name or acknowledge. Those rags, pieces of pain, leftovers, desires, rages, tears compose the essential ingredients for our fresh starts.

Our culture is permeated by words and phrases prompted by our long association with farm animals. A "cash cow" means a thing of value. A "sacred cow" means an important belief. The term "golden calf" appears in Exodus when Aaron makes a golden calf and puts an altar before it. God then tells Moses that his people have corrupted themselves by worshipping a golden calf instead of their God. Moses burns a calf, grinds it into powder, mixes it with water and makes people drink of it. Thus, the word has come to signify crass materialism, instead of worship.

A "chick" means a foolish young girl, "chicken" came to mean cowardly. "Which comes first—the chicken or the egg?"—is a common riddle. "Chicken feed," "hen-pecked," "hen party," "cocksure," and "bulldoze" are all phrases heard in daily life. I'm sure you can think of many others.

And the stories we tell! Our childhoods are imbued with fairy tales and the Mother Goose rhymes in which farm animals appear as teachers or companions. Beatrix Potter, E. B. White, Porky Pig cartoons created legends that are engrained in many of our hearts.

Farm animals were intimately connected to the call for sacrifice. Sacrifice appears to be a psychological need that in ancient times was expressed with symbolic animal offerings. Historians tell how early peoples asked the Holy Ones for rain, fertility, in short, survival and offered sacrifices to bargain with, appease, atone for wrongs, and express gratitude. Docile sheep were often used for sacrifice, while calves were considered too expensive to part with. Thus, the lamb became a suitable symbol for Jesus, who became known as the Lamb of God who taketh away the sins of the world.

Rambunctious goats came to be sacrificed to appease God's wrath over what humans thought was bad behavior. Thus, originated the word "scapegoat." The live goat, taking the blame for all the peoples' sins, was sent into the desert. If it survived, it meant God forgave them. In some cultures, even today, two people, usually a man and woman, are selected to bear the guilts of all the people. They are publicly paraded, then put in a pit and stoned to death.

But scapegoating exists all around us. It's in the tendency to "profile" people ethnically or by the clothes they wear. We blame others for our shortcomings or failures. Or we suffer from others who project onto us. If a goat appears in a dream, you might examine your attitudes and behavior.

Sacrifice lives on as an act we are still called upon to do. All of us at different points in our lives will have to "sacrifice" one job for another, one lover for another, one home for another. It may be that like sheep, we are following the herd, a collective idea, or a naïve sentimental attitude too much. The outer attachment will have to be broken in order for something fresh—a new direction, a new structure—to take place. The ancient principle that something must die in order for rebirth to occur still functions. In sleep-dreams the need for a sacrifice to be made in our lives may include images of an animal being killed in a primitive rite. It may be very hard for us to let go of what we love but the equally strong principle of change in life requires it.

Much lore in art and literature has been passed on regarding specific animals and archetypal acts. While I will touch on some of this lore regarding pigs, goats, and cattle, I urge you to explore more in mythology books. Following your own motifs is part of the journey of understanding your life.

In Neolithic pottery the Earth Goddess is represented as a sow. The pig was worshipped when women were entirely in charge of agriculture. Its rooting in the soil was like reaping and sowing. Pigs also grew fast and had many offspring, a sign of fertility.

In Greece, Demeter the Earth Goddess was pictured with pigs and barley. In Demeter's story her daughter Persephone falls into the Underworld. A pig falls in with her. Demeter spends her time searching for Persephone, and in the meantime her grief causes the crops to dry up. This interval became known as autumn and winter. When she is at last reunited with Persephone, spring comes with the renewal of all life forms. A sacrifice of the pig was considered very great for it was charged with her divine mystery. Pigs are still sacrificed in sacred ceremonies around the world.

The myths about pigs though are contradictory, depending upon cultures. Pigs were considered coarse and gluttonous by Jews, Islamics, and Chinese. In Egypt the pig was sacred to the Mother Goddess Isis but the black pig represented the dark side of Net, who swallowed Isis' son Horus' eye. Zeus was to have been suckled by a pig. To the Celt's eating pigs was like feasting on the gods.

Some dreams of pigs will be about stuffing ourselves and something needing to be eliminated. For instance, a woman mothers her own children and other people as though they are her children. When mothering turns into smothering or controlling the lives of others, she or he will need to sacrifice the pig. Such a dream will come, showing that the pig must die, meaning that the person must not parent others for a time, just as Demeter had to be parted from Persephone for half the year. Letting one's charges go is painful, so is leaving one who has been a good mother, but that dependency is a cord that must be cut or it will rot and poison both ends.

Another aspect is that of gluttony of food, alcohol, or drugs. In such addictions, we are probably seeking the spirit of the Great Mother, as we experience voracious need and insatiable longings for comfort. In essence, addictions are a spiritual problem. In yielding to the substance rather than the spirit, we give over to the dark side of consumption. But through the sacrifice of inner piggishness, we can enhance our spiritual being. Once we understand our avaricious emotional neediness, we can move into rebirth and redemption.

Goats have produced intense reactions, largely centered around the buck's ability to fertilize many females within short spans of time. Because as the-male goat matures, he emanates a strong odor, the term "old goat" has been applied to lecherous old men who smell bad. Since the goat was so popular among many pagan cultures, Christians depicted it as the Devil and made cloven hoofs its sign as part of their campaign to repress sexuality.

The more life-affirming Greeks, however, every spring celebrate the moving of the sap in the trees, the urge to copulate arising in the sheep and goats, and the readiness of the soil for seeding. People dress in goat skins and hang bells around their waists and dance in the streets. The god Pan symbolizes all this earthy energy. Many images show him with a man's head and chest, a goat's torso and legs, an engorged penis. He was mated to Athene, Penelope, and many archaic forms of the Goddess. He was the god of woods and pastures, the protector of shepherds and flocks. Often in dreams the quality of life that he personifies is dead and needs reviving.

The cow is an ancient symbol of the feminine. The Mother Goddess was worshipped as a female body with a cow's head and hoofs.

In predynastic Egypt, where the cow form of Hathor was adored, Hathor bore the face of the sky and the deep waters. She was the creator of the Milky Way. "Seek the Cow Mother" was written on the walls of the tombs of early kings. Hathor reigned until Isis came along and incorporated her imagery. In a statue her body is golden, covered with trefoils and quartrefoils that resemble the stars. Between her horns she bears the sun disks, wreathed by soaring flowery plumes. A young king kneels to drink from her udder. Her nourishment provides the sustenance that protects him on his journey to the next world, where she alone presides. She also embodied the pleasures of touch—art, singing, dancing.

While the cow was an epiphany of the goddess herself, the bull became a symbol of phallic power, though not a partner of the goddess for She was parthenogenic. The majesty and prowess of the bull were depicted in the caves of Lascaux, France, (ca.17,000–12,000 B.C.E.).

In a Sumerian myth (around 4–3000 B.C.E.) the Fertility Goddess Inanna and the Shepherd King Damuzi (shown as a bull), entreats him to "plow her vulva". When they copulate, vegetation springs up. At this time the balance between cow and bull, feminine and masculine energies, were equal.

Not to be overlooked is the instructive Buddhist story about the ten stages of attaining enlightenment. Known as the oxherding pictures, the ox (or bull or cow) represents the Self or soul. In the first picture a boy searches for it. He catches glimpses of it in nature, meditations, and imaginings. Eventually he mounts it but the animal is unruly; a struggle ensues as the boy tries to control it with ropes. When he drops the ropes, trusting in the instinctual and divine animal to lead, they proceed in harmony. Near the final stage, both disappear into nirvana. The boy returns as a humble man with blessed offerings.[79]

---

79. Based on a 15th century Chinese poem, one commentary may be found in Daisetz Suzuki's, *Manual of Zen Buddhism* (New York: Grove Press, 1960).

The parts of the cow are also symbolic. A cornucopia was the horn of plenty, filled with all the fruits of the soil. The inside of the cow was revered for its transformation of grass into abundant milk. The taking of milk from other species has been seen as a most intimate act. The Balinese still cremate a body in a cow-shaped coffin to signify the return to the womb of the "mother."

In countless beliefs, projected into art and language, humans used the qualities of domestic animals. A fortunate person indeed is one who dreams of a thriving populace in the barnyard with a good man or woman, enthusiastic and caring about the animals. Contentment is where the farm has sows with piglets, cows with calves, sheep, and goats, water and good pasture. Such an image means all is right in your world and psyche. This is the harmony we can attain if we correct the mistakes of the present.

HORSES: So Willing and Eloquent

A motif recurs in dreams: the horse screams to be released. The horse screams and screams. It rears and bucks, lunges at the line, the fence, any restraint. Tousled mane and tail whip like flags of freedom.

Postcards, calendars, TV commercials, movie logos show horses running free along beaches and cliffs of canyons, over meadows of red poppies—images that catch at our throat and tug at our longings. The power of legs gathered in a gallop, the rippling haunch muscles, double-barreled chest, arched neck, long head with large round eyes, flared nostrils, ears perked in attention or flattened in anger. Horses stir admiration for majesty in motion, the call to adventure, the memory of being wild and the ache to be so again.

But it has been a long long time since horses were truly wild. Millions of years ago as horses evolved (at first from animals the size of house cats), they once roamed this continent freely, but then 8–10,000 years ago largely died out. The continued existence of horses has depended upon their willingness to be of use to people—whether for farming, warring, hunting, traveling, performing. They were domesticated about 6000 years ago (well after dogs, sheep, goats, and cattle), and henceforth bred, fed and raised in captivity. (When they escape, they are just called "feral" because they are not believed to be descendants of truly wild species.) More than any other animal, horses greatly influenced the spread of civilization.

At the start horses were a prime source of meat and hides. But then the horse's energy, weight, and conformation—heart, lungs, legs, and hoofs—made it seem capable of so much more. They were first harnessed to carts and made to haul things. We don't know when they were first ridden but we do know that in the 5th c. A.D. the Chinese invented the stirrup and so riding for sure took place by then.

People harnessed the qualities of horses in order to be more mobile. A nomadic shepherd could only go so far on foot. Upon a horse, he could extend his reach. As horses thus enabled people to travel long distances, people could hunt more efficiently, graze their sheep and cattle more widely, and improve their plowing and cultivating of crops. People were also able to get about and meet with others, spreading political news and fostering educational centers.

Mounted on horses, men went to war up to and including World War I. For centuries military prowess was indicated by armies of men on decorated horses. Horses with stamina and intelligence were prized. Arabs fought each other regularly in the desert. The medieval romance of chivalry centered on armored knights astride heraldic horses. Sentiment held that horses carried their masters for the sake of king, country, and religion. Legions of horses died in this warfare. Now we still have police cavalries. The elegance and precision of dressage moves are based on military training.

Horses became a symbol of wealth. The best horses were bought and maintained by the richer classes, who originated the rituals of the foxhunt. Ever since saddles were put on horses, men raced them for their entertainment.

People can be very possessive and proud of their horses. In Iceland horses are treated almost as members of the family. They are so fiercely protected that no other breed has been allowed in or out since being introduced by Norsemen in AD 800.[80] Once exported, an Icelandic horse may not be allowed back in the country. Icelandic horses are renowned for their still smooth five gaits. They are small yet powerful, with friendly, well-balanced dispositions, perhaps because they are not trained to be ridden until the age of four and are so well esteemed.

Horses are the most fabulous of domestic animals, admired and loved by women as well as men. They've been the subject of paintings and sculptures since Paleolithic days. The only animal commonly ridden, it is

---

80. Janine Gordon, "A Horse of a Different Color," *Hemispheres* (June, 1994), p. 88.

exciting to settle onto their smooth backs, high from the ground, be carried fast, smell their sweat, feel the heat rising, listen to their snorts and tail swishing. They stir our dreams and imagination more than any other animal, like unrequited passion.

Capturing Horse Power in the Americas

Domesticated horses were brought to America by the Spaniards in the late 15th century. Historians say that without the horse, the Spaniards' conquests in the Americas would not have been possible.

Indians got hold of horses and soon adapted them to their needs for roaming the land and defending themselves. The Nez Perce Indians, for instance, are known for cultivating the Appaloosa with its bright spots, white hips, roan hair, and striped hoofs in a deep valley along the Palouse River in the (now) state of Washington. Descendants of these horses, derived from the Spanish stallions and mares, became the mustangs found throughout the west. Indians decorated their horses fancily. One of Black Elk's visions was of "a nation of horses dancing."

On the east coast the Puritans and early colonists brought horses for work over from Europe. The English were the first to organize a horse race—in 1664 at a place called Newmarket on Long Island. Horses were noteworthy in the Revolutionary and Civil Wars. They enabled people to migrate westward with covered wagons and stagecoaches. Horses and cowboys became icons. Western boots, jeans, vests, jackets are still the height of fashion, even worn by CEO's whose work takes them nowhere near horses. By 1920 some 25 million horses, including the graceful draft breeds—Percheron, Clydesdales, Shires, and Suffolks—worked on American farms. Now, of course, these horses have largely been replaced by machinery.

Throughout our history with horses some people have realized that horses will cooperate best when kindly treated. The best riders and trainers know that maintaining a good relationship involves frequent caresses, proper feeding, cleaning, talking, singing, and mutual respect. They rave about what they learn from horses. A prime example of how healing the bond is can be found in the grateful words of this woman who suffered from an inherited lung ailment:

> Not only is my Pony a great source of happiness and escape from the grueling upkeep of my health, but she is also part of my general physical and mental well-being. When I'm sick, just going up and hearing her munch on a carrot and seeing the delight on her face when I unwrap a mint for her brings me great happiness. In many instances she can tell when I am ill and need to slow down or stop.

Monty Roberts, now an older horseman, grew up on a ranch where the horses were "broken" by being hobbled and lashed. By observing horses, he noticed that they have their own way of communicating. When he told his father that he wanted to speak to the horses in their own language, his father beat him with a chain so badly he had to be hospitalized. That experience made him more determined to train horses in a softer, gentler way, a story which he described in his best-seller, *The Man Who Talked to Horses*.

He observed how horses communed among themselves, largely with body language. Always watchful, they need to feel protected. Like deer, they are flight animals and ready to bolt at a moment's notice. Humans as fight animals, the ones who pursue and conquer, have to achieve trust with horses in order for the relationship to work well.

Despite a few horse whisperers, many horses are subjected to great cruelties. Many are whipped bloody by irate riders. Or, left starving when someone no longer pays for their feed. Many are slaughtered and canned (meat exported largely to Europe, Japan, and Mexico.) No rules govern how much rest, food or water the doomed horses get. The livestock industry fights regulations because it fears that if horses get protections, cattle and other farm animals will too.

In the competitive world unsuccessful horses may not be tolerated. An example is the case of Tommy Burns, who was arrested for killing unwanted race horses, at the behest of owners who wanted to collect insurance money on them. He said, "I did it for the money. For the owners it was rotten cheapness at its worst." He carried out his nefarious task by first secretly cracking one horse's leg with a crowbar. The horse screamed in pain, while Tommy and the owner ostentatiously called the vet to end its life. The insurance company was told that the horse broke its leg in the rain. In order to convince insurance companies, Tommy usually killed horses with an industrial-sized extension cord and a couple of alligator clips. He would attach one of the clips to a horse's ear and the other to its anus. He then plugged the extension cord into an outlet and stepped back as the horse dropped dead. Electrocution left few if any telltale signs and mostly resembled colic. Tommy claimed that he would have to get drunk whenever he did this.[81]

Such treatment lives on in our collective memories.

DREAMS & VISIONS OF HORSES

When we ride or look at horses, circuits in our minds and bodies connect and flash. Because horses appear in thoughts, wishes, daydreams, night dreams, yearnings, aroused feelings, and inspirations, they deserve to be listened to, for they speak of our life, individual and collective. If ignored, the horses will appear in dreams neighing insistently.

In interpreting your dreams, think of your own associations to horses. It does not help to impose dogmatic symbols, such as a black horse represents death and a white one life. Better to give priority to your own memories, ideas and reflections and let them lead you to search among the varying legends from other cultures to enhance their meaning. The range of examples begins with the magnificent horse paintings in cave art.

The pounding of the horses' hooves upon the ground made people believe that horses were in touch with the chthonic powers of the underworld. In fables and legends horses were depicted as clairvoyant, often giving a timely warning to their masters. They were associated with foresight, understanding, intensity, passion, and instinctual knowledge. When blacksmiths later forged horseshoes in the shape of crescent moons,

---

81. Don Terry, "On Killing Horses for Money: A Craftsman's Dirty Secrets," *New York Times* (Sept. 5, 1993), p.1.

these became talismans against ill fortune and are posted on barns, houses, and ships even today.

In India the horse was akin to the wind, waves, and sun. In Vishnu's last appearance he was to ride a white horse named Kalki and bring peace and salvation. For 2000 years tales of erotic horned horses or unicorns, representing spiritual penetration, emerged from Asia, Persia, and Europe.

Hindu queens impersonated the Goddess by inserting a dead horse's penis between their legs, calling upon its seed for the benefit of the land and people. Such a wedding spawned the horse-gods known in the Aegean as centaurs, who joined the power and speed of the horse with the intelligence and emotion of humans.

Around 1185, Irish rituals recorded that the king would copulate with a mare in a kind of marriage vow to the land. Then the mare would be slaughtered and cooked. The king would bathe in the broth, drink it with his hands, and eat some of her flesh. All of this was designed to take in the numerous aspects of the horse: a blend of abundance, nourishment, fertility, and potency.[82]

A modern woman dreamed that <u>she and her mother looked at wedding photo of her niece, and she is standing with her horse. Her face looks happy. Her horse is a shiny bay with a narrow white blaze. Her mother says, "why would she have her horse in her wedding photo?" The woman answered, "Because the horse is her lover" (and then adds embarrassed), "and also her best friend." Her mother accepts in silence.</u> The numinosity of this image harkens back to the ancient marriage ritual that in this case takes place in the woman's psyche.

The horses that carried men into battle were associated with Mars, the god of war. Northern Europeans made horses essential to the funerals of great warriors. Hence the riderless black horse symbolized the horse's carrying the leader's ghost to heaven. Sometimes the horse was sacrificed too and buried with a dead hero. On the other hand, Buddha gave up horses as a sign of abandoning the martial way.

---

82. Wendy Doniger O'Flaherty, *Women, Androgynes and Other Mythical Beasts* (Chicago: University of Chicago Press, 1980), p.152. Also a Nordic practice.

Many stories surround Poseidon, King of the Sea, who, taking the shape of a stallion, mated with Medusa in the temple of Athene. She was infuriated at the profanation and turned Medusa's hair into snakes. Medusa then represented untempered, flooding emotional energy. When Perseus decapitated Medusa, he gave her head to Athene who wore it as a shield. In other words, wisdom mastered that fierce energy but needed it for protection in battle. From the blood that escaped during the beheading sprang Pegasus, the winged horse, who became a favorite divine spirit representing the poetic aspect of human nature.

Dreams or visions often facilitate the movement of creative ideas from the unconscious depths to a state that consciousness can master. Such ideas seem like bursts of inspiration, ranging from brief to long visions. On these treasured occasions one seems to ride the muse.

The horses that have reverberated throughout history and myths are far too numerous to list. I want to show how important horses have been to a few people in quite different ways. Maybe these examples will spark insights of your own.

First is Sir Laurens van der Post, a World War II hero and author, who had once lived among the Kalahari Bushmen, been a prisoner of war, and was devoted to the interconnectedness of all life. He was afflicted with cancer in his old age. Suddenly one day he remembered a horse he had in childhood, which led to a healing experience that he documented in *About Blady*. He wrote:

> The emotions of this recall were so intense, despite the seventy years of silence in between the experience we shared and the present, that I felt more sure than ever that the race against cancer could not have been won had it not been for similar emotions and energies of spirit stored up in the soul of man by his timeless association with the horse.[83]

His life as an old man at the time seemed impoverished and drab compared to his time with the horse. When he asked Fredy Meier, a Swiss

83.   Laurens van Der Post, *About Blady* (New York: William Morrow, 1991), p. 92.

Jungian analyst, if his recollections of the horse's energy could heal him, Meier answered, "yes," adding "Have you forgotten the Centaur, the horse-man Chiron? He was the great healer of antiquity. He healed gods and heroes and trained Asclepius (the god of health and healing), also Achilles."[84] Thus was van der Post led from his personal memories of his horse to making use of the healer, Chiron, as an inner wisdom figure.

Deborah Butterfield is an internationally collected artist, who rides, trains, and sculpts horses. She says, "Horses are the format I've chosen for interpreting my thoughts." Her commitment is like being "married to the horse" because it involves loyalty and patient learning.[85]

As a young child, she says, horses "filled my eye as the most important thing in my life." As she grew up and got more familiar with horses, she at first thought she wanted to become a veterinarian. A severe car accident gave her both a lasting awareness of the potential closeness of death at any minute as well as a settlement that financed her way through college and her first horse. Soon she began making and then teaching art. Her first medium was clay. When she made the transition to horses, one of her first pieces was a pair of ceramic hooves.

As her sculpted horses sold well, she was able to build a sleek modern barn and indoor arena, where she enables a small group of people to board horses, practice dressage, and participate in occasional clinics. She also has provided opportunities to handicapped people to ride. In all these ventures she has paid close attention to horses and learned much about their ways and manners.

She is keenly aware of how horses seek to be in dialogue with us. When we sit upon their backs, we feel a sense of being carried through space, in a way that we can't get from our own legs. The horses know our weaknesses but also our leadership skills. Deborah compares working with them to dancing with different individuals who can't talk to you. Much has to do with body language. Rider and horse fumble around but when the right move is found, both feel a certain happiness.

---

84. *Ibid.*, p. 129.

85. Quotes from my interview with Deborah Butterfield.

In a herd mares are the decision makers, because they must protect the foals; the stallions simply fertilize. Horses don't need to be at the top of a hierarchy but they like security. Deborah finds these lessons also apply to being a parent. The rules need to be clear and firm. "When you train horses and do things consistently, they express themselves more fully."

In her art Deborah expands on the impressions she gets from being around horses. While her horses seem to be true to their essences, in actuality her standing horses are taller than they would be. She uses the horse's body as an abstract rectangular canvas that she can paint with mud, sticks, steel, aluminum, or bronze. One sculpture is of a horse standing with head bent, surrounded and partially hidden by tall thin sticks. The artist speaks about the horse basking in rays of sunlight. One of her reclining horses is made of metal and wood and brick dust; it is pierced with jagged wood stakes—it is called "Rosary," pierced like a Catholic saint.

The sculptural materials—wood, steel, wire—become more than their subject. As an artist, Deborah Butterfield has had the skill to express her own transcendent thoughts and evoke deep feeling responses in us. While making her statements, she also wants people to feel empathy for horses. "I'm trying to get the viewer to project himself or herself into the form of the horse. I want people to actually be able to crawl into that shape and inhabit it, and to perceive in a different way." Her intent to present the horse's perspective on our world is a political act.

Deborah Butterfield's soul work with horses is documented in marvelous sculptures that can be seen and touched. Now shamelessly I will tell about my own soul work with horses, which is less tangibly expressed in works of art but equally valuable in the artwork of my life. You may have your own soulful story.

When I was a child, absorbing the pictures of beautiful Arabians in books, I did not realize they would enchant me for life. The story of *Black Beauty* made me cry when this plucky mare was owned by harsh people, and exult when she was restored to a field of lush grass. (A side effect was its instruction on the changing fortunes of fate.) Walter Farley's many *Black Stallion* books showed that a child could be the companion of a tempestuous creature. While the stallion could break away at any moment, it would hold still, even want to. Rapport was possible!

As a child, with dread and anticipation, I accompanied my father to a stable in a dingy building in downtown Chicago to learn how to ride. It took an Austrian trainer of Arabian dressage horses to help me overcome my fears and become a rider. Overcoming the fear and learning to work as a team with the horse are huge steps for a rider.

While everyone has their own entry into the realm of horses, I was brought up in the saddle horse scene, which consisted of show horse competitions in equitation, three- and five-gaited classes. In the south and west there are rodeos, and in the east hunters and jumpers. Not to mention the racing "thoroughbreds" and polo matches. Each sphere has its own protocol, prized animals, clothing.

Week after week, I'd go to the stable. I was in the animal world, seeking escape from my human life—school and parents—happy in jeans or shorts, bringing carrots and apples to the horses, learning to groom them, and getting to know their personalities. There was Safety who'd been scarred in a fire. Dark Zorro steamed with energy; after an hour on him, his neck would be lathered like soap. Citation, a red chestnut with a white lightning streak, was dignified and reliable, always alert.

Caught up in horse shows, I longed for my own horse to show in equitation classes. I cajoled my father into buying, first Becky Sue, a sweet, pretty, and docile mare who after awhile bored me. We sold and exchanged her for five-gaited Fancy Rose. Black with long flowing mane and tail, she was as close to "the black stallion" as I would ever get.

While her temper remained consistently calm and reasonable, she trotted and cantered with pent-up liveliness. I thought at times she could easily slip out of my control, a feeling that seemed exciting. I took great pleasure in caring for her big beautiful body. Before and after a ride, I would curry her, bringing up clouds of dust from her skin. Then using the stiff-bristled corn brush and the softer "finishing" brush, I'd make her coat glossy. I'd brush softly around her ears and eyes, talking to her. Slowly I'd separate the long tangled hairs of her tail and comb them with a metal comb. If we were in a show, I'd also put black shoe polish on her hooves and dress myself in black jodhpurs with a white, long-sleeved shirt (French cuffs) and black topcoat and derby hat.

I am ashamed to say that I also subjected my horses to chains wrapped around their ankles, which presumably would make them lift their knees up higher in an effort to fling them off, the aim being to induce high action. Before shows I put tail sets on them at night—dreadful harnesses designed to keep vertical the first six inches of their tail, which had been cut surgically. The harness wrapped around their chest and along the lengths of their bodies. Despite all the artificial contraptions, Fancy Rose would not be a big winner because she was not top caliber. The consistent winners then cost over $10,000.

The days of showing Fancy Rose came to an end suddenly when my mother married a man from Texas and wanted to move us there. In the land of quarter horses and rodeos, Fancy Rose had no place to be shown. But she became much more valuable as a companion during this hard transition. When I rode her, I'd sing songs: "My Wild Irish Rose;" "I see the moon, the moon sees me, God bless the moon, God bless thee." She embodied all that was warm and familiar to me.

And yet there were times when I—a teenager—neglectfully let the grain stand too long in her box so that maggots were born under it. Such an incident would haunt me later.

When I went east to college, I had to sell her. I can't remember to whom. As for Black Beauty, such is the fate of most animals. We cannot remember—or do not even know—what happens to them. But I found the discarded horse returned to me in dreams, carrying potent insights.

Riding a horse—whether in a paddock, over jumps, across rangeland, along forest trails—is one kind of pleasure. Just as real and important are the horses of our imaginations. Although I no longer had a horse to ride, they infiltrated my existence. Whenever I wrote the word "house" or "horse," I unconsciously inserted an "r" or "u," invariably writing "hourse." The horse is my house, where I truly live.

Over a decade after college, when my own children grew to riding age, I eagerly introduced them to horses, as if their lives depended on knowing them. My son, thrown early, remained resistant, even though he is a strong athlete. My daughter, who learned to jump horses, drew close. Seeking to avoid the show circuit, we bought a house with a barn where she could know the pleasure of just caring for horses and riding them on trails nearby.

Her first, Malarkey, was a gray jumper (common in New England). Although small, he was feisty. In the spring, when the sap started to run in trees and soil became soft and the scent of fertility was in the air, he would jump the fence of the paddock and have a fine old time clopping down the street. All the horses in the neighborhood would start neighing to each other, like an ancient call to herd and gallop away from humans.

In the 70's my daughter and I tried something new. We bought a young whitish-gray Arabian, who at four years old was still green, thus giving my daughter an opportunity to learn something about a horse as she trained it. This Arabian was named after a story by Anais Nin, in which Tishnar was the name of the ideal lover. He had the characteristic majestic head and friendly disposition of Arabians. He would hang his head with big round eyes over the fence and watch for our comings and goings from the house, softly nickering if he was looked at.

Some say that girls like horses as a prelude to sexual awakening with a male. The British Peter Shaffer wrote the play "Equus," in which a boy stabs horses' eyes with a stake. This play takes place in England, where horses are the basis of a sophisticated, genteel sport, and social manners are rigidly observed. The boy desires desperately to ride away from his repressed Christian life but is so fearful of doing so that he seeks to obliterate the horses, on whom he has projected his uncontrollable sexual desires.

We want the vitality the horse presents in potentia, not bridled or fenced in. We want and fear the wildness badly, but in our misperceptions may attack the animal for our failures.

I have often dreamed that Tishnar wants to be free. He's tied to a fencepost, pulls back, breaks the rope, and makes a mad dash for the open gate. Or, he pushes against weak fence rails of a paddock. I threaten him back and put up barbed wire. He urinates in mockery, and I know he'll break through but I'm scared. In another variation on this theme, a herd of horses runs around frantically, looking for a way out. These dreams came at the times when as a responsible wife and mother, I struggled for free time to put into creative work. If I let the discipline go, I feared the order I maintained would fall apart.

In a meditation then came the phrase, "Riding my horse without spurs." That meant managing myself and others with loose reins, sitting firm, but directing lightly, with an attitude of give and take. To achieve this rapport requires concentration, gathering in the tension, not digging in with barbs. The mantra also meant letting other people and work tasks proceed at their own pace and continuing on despite the bruises.

I dreamed of <u>my son on a big black horse, which is acting up and scaring him</u>. I have observed that my son represents for me my young masculine self making its way in the world—the young innocent wanting to become heroic. Part of me was scared of a dark and earthy force inside me. Although uncertain and tentative, I knew I needed to bring that element into my family, my work, my presence.

One day weighted down by the blanket of duties and inner conflicts, I wrote out a fantasy in which I merged with two horses. One was a magnificent winged stallion with a long flaxen mane and tail that touches the ground. He pranced around a shaggy, gray mare who is curious but unreceptive. She eats, runs away. He joins her and soon as they run together, an invisible fire ignites between them. Then he almost flies toward her, wings beating, hooves pounding. She opens her petals for him. They sink into the mud, darkness, and blend beings. In this rough union, the Earth and he and she became one.

Writing down this act of imagination worked psychological changes. First, I absorbed much of the feral horse's down and dirty energy. I attained more inner fire and will. Then through the symbolic union with the male horse, I received the potency of the masculine spirit. This inner experience is linked to the archaic Celtic and Gallic rituals mentioned earlier, in which the King or Queen would copulate with the horse. Such an inner event changes one's way of being in life. It went a long way toward strengthening my resolve to attain inmost desires, while undoing former constrictions.

Eventually Tishnar too was sold, when my daughter went off to college. A year or so later we tried to visit him but the family had split up and moved on, whereabouts unknown. So Tishnar joined the legacy of Black Beauty. But Tishnar remains a central character in my journal work. Whenever I do not give my inner vitality enough food or nurturance, a dream comes to remind me of caring for my power and energy. My life brings me to new crossroads repeatedly and his image urges me in unfathomable ways to commit to the path I desire. He personifies the genuine and invincible still small voice within.

I find I am in the best state when I maintain a vision of a horse standing on a cliff, nose to the air, sniffing the wind, skin so vibrant it trembles, ready to take off in any direction.

PETS: Dogs & Cats

In the tree of life cats and dogs split apart about 40 million years ago and followed different lines of development. Cats became stealthy hunters, dogs feisty runners. Domestication inspired their human owners to bring them into their homes rather than board them outside. For the most part, we stopped eating them. We made them into friends and made eye contact with them, which wild animals cannot allow. Pets care about our love or approval, wild animals don't.

People hold positive and negative perspectives on pets. The negative one is expressed by people like ecologist and author Paul Shepard, who views pets as the outcome of unrestricted genetic engineering. As he sees it, people of long ago captured wild animals, killing those who were aggressive and breeding the more tractable ones. As the resulting animals became docile and servile, they were seen as toys and given to children to play with. Shepard calls pets "civilized paraphernalia." In the negative view, pets represent the ultimate in human control of nature, "a perversion of biological evolution."[86] Some people now pay tens of thousands of dollars to have their pets cloned.

The positive view is that pets bring us to a higher level of happiness than life without them. They open us to their way of perceiving things. We engage with them in play and communication. Often regarded as part of the family, pets make us less lonely, providing companionship for ourselves, our elders and children.

Studies overwhelmingly show that living with pets is beneficial to our health and morale. In talking quietly to cats and dogs, touching, stroking

---

86. Paul Shepard, *The Others: How Animals Made Us Human* (Washington, D.C.: Island Press, 1996), p. 144.

them, our blood pressure lowers, and we become gentler and more relaxed. People with severe anxieties as in Alzheimer's disease or autism, improve. The blind and deaf are aided in their daily chores.

Although many of us love our pets, that doesn't mean we always treat them well. The problem comes from not appreciating their gestures or sounds, thus not recognizing their genuine needs or respecting their motives. Some think of pets as backward and foolish in comparison with us and berate them when their behavior does not suit our expectations. Author and trainer Vicki Hearne said that the animals' "first right, the right from which all others follow, for them and for us, is the right to be believed in."[87]

When people domesticated animals, they made them dependent on served food for their survival. The unwritten golden rule of domestication was that henceforth we would protect these animals. That has not proved to be the case though. We do not yet take collective responsibility for domestic animals. Many pets are starved, left behind when families moved, kicked out when no longer wanted, shot at for fun. They end up at the animal pound, which is somewhat like a concentration camp in that millions of cats and dogs are euthanized there annually.

CATS: *Royal Paupers*

Cats descend from the big lions and tigers. Despite being smaller in size, pound for pound they are very strong. They hunt but they do not work together as well as lions do. Cats show most attention when stalking and pouncing on live prey. From birth on, they enjoy the sport of it more than the catch. Cats thrive on fresh meat, are not vegetarians, except for reveling in catnip and occasional leaves or grass for vitamins.

As we know, cats can be remarkably still and quiet. Approaching life with reserve and caution, they put their feet-pads down gently, often leaving no print. (Dogs by comparison are more anxious and lively; they leave footprints.) They will lie curled up with tails tucked, paws folded inward, unresponsive to being called.

---

87. Vicki Hearne, *Adam's Task* (New York: Vintage, 1987), p. 266.

Cats watch us closely. Many owners say cats are sensitive to their moods and respond in remarkable ways. They can sulk and withdraw when they see your suitcase pulled out on the bed, as if they have to protect themselves while you are gone. They know when to jump in your lap or lie cradled in your arms with a paw resting on your cheek. They like to be stroked, not for "doing" things as dogs do, but just for the satisfaction of "being."

Their intelligence includes their ability to comfort pain and grief. They understand what objects are for—like when you turn the doorknob or approach the can opener. We know they dream and have memories.

Unlike dogs, cats refuse to be approved of or disapproved. They generally will not tolerate behavioral researchers' attempts to make them do things for food rewards. It's hard to manipulate a cat!

The selective breeding of cats has led to a variety of features. Tending to have coloration drawn from the landscape, Egyptian cats were known to be reddish or yellowish. Tabby cats were derived in Old Baghdad to imitate the stripes and water marks of silk. The British cultivated neat and sturdy shorthaired cats. Not liking gray cats, people made soft blue ones, finding pleasure in the chiaroscuro and silkiness of their fur.

The evolution of cats is inextricably bound to the history of human civilization. Ancient Egypt is the generally acknowledged cradle of the first tamed cats, around 2600 B.C.. These cats were highly respected for their many charms. They were used in the hunting of ducks and fish. The Egyptians, having invented long-term storage of grain in silos, found cats to be avid protectors of their granaries, where mice and rats gathered.

By the XX-XXIIth dynasties cats became totems for their protective and feminine qualities. Women wanted to copy the cat's concerted gaze, slanting eyes, supple loins, noble posture and eroticism. Bastet (or Bast) was a cat-headed goddess, often shown with kittens. She was a lover of pleasure, music and dance. Cats were embalmed when they died. Anyone who killed a cat was liable to death penalty.

As agricultural societies spread, cats were stolen and then bred by the Arabs, Greeks, and eventually Europeans, Indians, and Japanese. An interesting story says that cats don't appear in the zodiacs of China or

Japan, because at the death of Buddha, when all the animals were present, a cat killed a rat, and killing was against Buddha's precepts.

Cats were instrumental in the settling of America, as they saved food from rats and the people from plagues. Considered precious commodities, they were bought for gold and listed in wills.

Cats' low point in popularity was caused by Christians in the medieval period in Europe and 17th c. in America. Probably because of the sacred value attached to them by earlier matriarchal cultures, these Europeans conjectured that cats were the spawn of Satan, their howling was of the devil. Cats, especially black, were said to be able to change form into witches. As a result, witch hunts in Europe and colonial America led to vast numbers of cats being murdered. Terrified cats would be put in wicker baskets and burned. Many were skinned alive. Of course, the women associated with the cats were burned too. (Think about the origin of the expression, "There is more than one way to skin a cat.")

Now cats are under attack for their predatory qualities. Not only do cats hunt rodents, but they also go after baby rabbits, small reptiles, and birds. Millions of birds are reported killed by cats annually. Some people concerned with the dwindling population of birds worldwide have become very angry about cats' roles. They want people to keep their housecats inside all the time.

The biggest problem—for cats and birds—is the abandonment of cats. Then they become "feral," driven to survive by their wits. Careful estimates put feral cats at 40 million in number.[88] These cats live in poverty and hardship. Most groups agree that spaying and neutering all cats, except those that can be cared for, is necessary to reduce their population.

DOGS: *Wagging Tails*

Dogs face similar problems. While at least 58 million of them are owned in the U.S., several million a year are abandoned and then killed in pounds.[89] Dogs too should be spayed or neutered unless cared for. These

---

88. Jon Luoma, "Catfight," *Audubon Magazine* (New York: July 1997), p. 88.
89. "When Your Pet is Seriously Ill," *Parade Magazine* (March 23, 1997).

animals, who are so willing to be our friends and in need of our care, are often subjected to our inner darkness.

Dogs inherited a number of qualities from their ancient progenitor, the wolf. They still maintain some wolflike traits, such as their sense of play and loyalty and scent-marking.

Records from Ancient Egypt, around 2900 B.C., show Greyhounds to be one of the earliest types, designed for use in pack hunting. Mastiff-type dogs were developed for guarding and fighting. Eskimo dogs for hard labor. As the principles of breeding were mastered and refined over the generations, dogs' juvenile traits, such as big eyes and short legs, were accentuated. The Chinese short-faced, miniatures Pug and Pekingese are examples. Thought to be a protective asset, barking was also maintained through breeding. No other species of animal has such a high degree of variation in hair length, ears, tails, skull and jaw shape. All breeds from the Chihuahua to St. Bernard, Great Dane to Yorkshire Terrier, are included, making logical classification difficult for all concerned. While there are hundreds of recognized dog breeds now, they are dwindling.

With olfactory areas 14 times larger than ours, dogs smell 100 times better than we do. The wetness of their noses heightens their sensitivity. They can see better at night than we do and, since their eyes are on the sides of their heads, they have a wider range of vision. They can hear things from four times the distance than we can, especially the higher frequencies. Their ability to distinguish among frequencies helps them recognize their owner's footsteps or car from afar. Dogs know the smell of fear. When sensing others, they are very aware of states of mind inside the physical body. They've been known to obey an owner's order while it was still a thought, before it was verbally expressed.

It's common knowledge that dogs' panting helps them control their temperature by evaporating moisture that dissipates heat. Less well known is fact that the bottoms of their paws are the location of their only sweat glands. Consequently, in hot weather dogs may leave damp footprints.

Dogs are lively communicators. Their tails are used to express feelings—they wag, droop, stiffen, and tuck. Dogs also smile. We see it when their faces relax, their ears are low, eyes half shut, lips soft and parted, and chin high. Their whole bodies wriggle with joy. They lie on their backs, exposing their bellies, in acts of submission. They drop down on their forelegs in a bow to invite play.

Elizabeth Marshall Thomas wrote *The Hidden Life of Dogs* to describe her observations of eleven dogs and what they pursue on their own if left to their own devices. At night when her dogs were out, she followed them. She found that they navigated through traffic with ease. Their main interest appeared to be not a search for sex, people, food, or hunting but to find other dogs. She believes that they have a memory from their wolf ancestry of circling and dominating each other. (Interestingly, the writer Sherwood Anderson once described walking at dusk in a forest and seeing 12–20 dogs running in a circle in a clearing. He felt transported to a primitive world.) The dogs would establish rank immediately, like wolves.

Think of ourselves too when we gather in groups, to what extent do we make comments and connections to establish our status? What makes us feel low-down or superior to others? Do we not defer to those we consider higher in rank?

Many observers believe that dogs' greatest desire is to have a sense of belonging, to give and receive love. Another great desire is to do work. Border collies protect sheep. (or anything that moves). Rescue dogs search avalanches for victims. Dogs in war carry messages, find the wounded, go through tough basic training, even parachuting. Many a war veteran has wept over the brave deeds of their dogs. Dogs have been trained to sniff out drugs. They ward off petty crime on streets, in parks, at universities. They've been actors in movies. They are highly therapeutic to sick people, prisoners, the handicapped, showing a great deal of patience and tolerance when they get confused signals. They bring relief in crisis situations. As a Red Cross spokesman said, "The dogs have worked the most wonders with men and boys, the tough type of people who don't necessarily know how to let go and show emotion." Dogs, like people, get great satisfaction from doing difficult things well. But most family dogs don't get near enough opportunities to live up to their potential.

Doggy qualities have influenced our conflicted treatment of them throughout history. On the one hand, they were domesticated very early because as they hung around human settlements and their garbage, people recognized their positive qualities. Their tendency to bark and ward off intruders, their comradeship, and their ability to sniff out game and to be used to help carry loads seemed great advantages. Dogs' sensory capacities amplified humans' reach. Once upon a time to own dogs became a sign of wealth.

But dogs were also eaten—for example, by the Mayas and Aztecs, as well as in the South Pacific islands where there was a lack of game. Dogs were also consumed and relished by the Lewis and Clark expedition crew (except for Clark) who explored the lands west of the Mississippi. This, despite the fact that Newfoundlands were helpful in protection against charging buffalos.

In some cultures, for instance, observations of dogs' eating corpses and their strange reacting to rabies made them seem loathsome and vile. Among Asians dog saliva is an extreme form of pollution. In Indonesia mongrels with scabby hips and dangling tumors roam the streets and are regarded as reincarnated criminals. The way males relentlessly pursue and slather over a female in heat (perhaps caught in a long vagina-penis lock), lick their genitals and anus, mount peoples' legs, chase and kill other animals led to their having a reputation as "hounds of hell." From this line of thought, it came to be slanderous to call someone a "dog."

Regardless of our attitudes, dogs have defended and rescued countless people in dangerous circumstances. Their attachment to humans has lasted beyond death. When an owner dies, dogs have been known to sit by the grave until they expire. Such co-dependence we would not tolerate for our own kind, but it is not reproved in dogs.

An Intimate Relationship

As this history with cats and dogs has shown, we have an intimate relationship with them, for better or worse. They live in our rooms, sleep in some of our beds. Keeping them also has meant that we must provide for their elimination needs, certainly an inconvenience that many willingly adapt to. Some of us surely enjoy being the masters, the alphas, of our pets, albeit the relationship is unequal for they must accept our conditions.

They can rebel up to a point with incessant barking or meowing, scratching and biting. But as with our human relationships, we can make the shared intimacy more or less harmonious and productive, depending on our mutual appreciation of each other's qualities and capacities.

A contemporary expression of gratitude comes from Gary Kowalski in *The Souls of Animals*:

> So my dog is sort of guru. When I become too serious and preoccupied, he reminds me of the importance of frolicking and play. When I get too wrapped up in abstractions and ideas, he reminds me of the importance of exercising and caring for my body. On his own canine level, he shows me that it might be possible to live without inner conflicts or neuroses: uncomplicated, genuine, and glad to be alive.[90]

In bonding we talk to and confide in our pets, display their photographs, buy them special clothes and toys. In the last 25 years people have become more willing than ever to pay a great deal for their pets' health care and insurance. It is not unheard of for an owner to pay several thousand dollars for an organ transplant, open-heart surgery, urinary tract operation, orthodontics, kidney dialysis, and even tranquilizers. Support groups have formed to help those whose pets have died.

Here is an excerpt from the text of a woman's paid notice in the newspaper when her dog died. Jo Shields, a graphic designer, took her German Shepard to work every day.

> Often seen about town carrying books to the library, or perhaps a cup of coffee up Main Street, most had to admit he was a gentleman of great resourcefulness and uncompromising style. (He enjoyed fielding phone calls, for instance, with the message that he couldn't come to the phone because he was tied up.) His humor combined with an intense desire to please won him a

---

90. Gary Kowalski, *The Souls of Animals* (New Hampshire: Stillpoint Publishing, 1991), p. 2.

ribbon or two in his day and the love of his friends, clients, doctors and family. We miss your gracious manners and most gentle wit, dear Mikey. And we'll always remember what a wonderful "person" you were.

Some people seek in pets a closeness that they can't find with other people. Time and again people say that it is less stressful to be with their cat or dog than other persons. The animal is always there, unbetraying, seemingly faithful.

J.Allen Boone wrote in *Kinship of All Life* about Strongheart, a remarkable German Shepard whom he took care of for friends. The dog had been highly trained in the military and was brought to Hollywood to be in films. When the dog arrived, he inspected the house and grounds, opening and closing doors to let himself out. Strongheart insisted on getting up and going to bed at certain times. One day just as Boone was thinking about taking a day off from work, Strongheart read his mind and got out his hiking clothes. After having been repeatedly amazed by the dog, Boone decided to learn from him. He admitted that despite Strongheart's fame, he had still thought of him as a lower creature but when he changed his perspective, he began to see him as a spiritual teacher. Strongheart loved to go to the top of a mountain and sit there rapt, as if he was meditating on the cosmos. Boone found himself acquiring more peace and contentment when with him. The dog taught him the "art of living abundantly and happily in the present tense regardless of circumstances."[91]

A minister, who with her husband cares for at least 20 pets at a time in her home, along with two adopted children, does not feel stressed. Instead, active in a national animal ministry as well as her human one, she emphasizes how she learns from them so much about unconditional acceptance.

Cleveland Amory turned his intimate, empathetic feelings for animals, especially cats, into programs that benefit abused animals. He created the

---

91.   J. Allen Boone, *Kinship of All Life* (San Francisco: HarperSanFranciso, 1954), pp. 73-4.

Fund for Animals, and a couple of his books are *The Cat Who Came For Christmas* and *The Best Cat Ever*. An anecdote that illustrates his appreciation for the bonding of humans and their pets concerns the time when his mother was dying. For days she had not recognized her husband or anyone else. Amory brought into the hospital, despite protests from the staff, two dogs she'd loved. She reached out for them and smiled, then died the next day. Amory is an example of someone who did not just enjoy the benefits animals offered him, but made a lasting commitment to give something back.

We could be better companions and teachers, and sometimes "parents" to pets if we understood them more. We guess at pets' expressions and motives, sometimes wrongly. The more knowledge of animal behavior we have, the better are our interpretations. Pets make erroneous projections about us too. For instance, when a dog with a bone menaces us, the dog actually assumes we want the dirty old thing. We both project our own wishes onto each other.

Educating pets, especially dogs, is part of caring. The approach we take is often mirrored in our relationship with one another. We may be over-controlling or too passive (the equivalent being parents who can never say no have children who then whine constantly to get what they want.) Sharp corrections to pets and children are seen by some as strict and mean. But a disciplined trainer views nagging, coaxing tugs, puerile "good doggy's" or "good dear's," and bribes as demeaning, dishonest, and ultimately cruel. Dogs as well as children who don't receive firm guidelines become mean and snappish.

Maurice Sendak, the artist who has specialized in understanding the often submerged feelings of children (a few of his books are *Where the Wild Things Are, Outside Over There*, and *Dear Mili*), realized how much his relationship with his dog helps him understand himself better. Here are some of his comments. He begins by acknowledging his tendency to lose his temper with his dog:

> I see how many unpleasant aspects of my nature have to be repressed simply because I love him.….When you see your dog

cowering away from you, just as you likely did with your own parents, it forces you to look at yourself....Socially unacceptable behavior occurs because you are now dealing with a nonverbal creature and reliving, perhaps, a nonverbal moment form your own past....The relationship I share with him is incredibly intense and basic. He shares my room, he shares my bed, he shares my every thought.

I connect with him in a most crucial way that I don't with other people. Since I'm an artist who really thrives on early memory, (my) main talent is to mine this thing, and to handle it quite honestly, without softening it or holding it up in a rosy light...I have one subject, which is childhood, and I have one intention before I kick the bucket and that's to...really dig down to where the subsoil is. And Runge (his dog) is my most intimate companion in this project, because I relate to him in this nonverbal way. We journey together.[92]

DREAMS & VISIONS OF DOGS AND CATS

Writers and artists have lavishly expended their imaginations on cats and dogs. Edward Lear's "Owl and the Pussy-cat," Lewis Carroll's Cheshire Cat in *Alice in Wonderland*, and T.S. Elliot's Jellicle Cats are some favorites. The writer Colette once posed for a self-portrait, lying with arms outfront in the position of a cat. Some favorite visions of dogs are found in Jack London's *White Fang*, the Lassie television programs, Charles M. Schulz' Snoopy. Both dogs and cats are companions in numerous paintings and photographs.

The daily presence of pets means that they are the most likely animals to be used in dreams to illustrate certain issues in our personal lives. Since dreams compensate for our conscious state of mind, usually the animal shows us a conflict we dimly recognize. In order to correct our course of action, we first need to become aware of it.

---

92.   Monks of New Skete, *How to Be Your Dog's Best Friend* (Boston: Little, Brown & Co., 2002).

A common motif is <u>looking for a dog</u>. We know how dogs trot along sidewalks, smelling this and that, greeting people, joining other dogs. With their tails high in the air and wagging, they look eager, curious, hungry. So in such a dream of looking for a dog, one possibility is that you could use a dose of the freedom and spontaneous wandering that a dog has. You need to be more of a loyal companion to your self, the way a dog is called "man's best friend." If you are not, the situation will get worse, and you're likely to have a dream of a dog lying near death or already dead. Then serious consideration will have to be paid to how in your life you are excluding the expression of friendly, eager curiosity in your life and make changes. On the other hand, it's a very good sign when you and your dream dog gaily stroll along.

Dreams also frequently show animals in need of rescue, and the dream will be specific as to how. The dream may show the dog wounded in the leg or tied up and choking. A wound means that particular spot needs care. The leg has to do with the ability to move. Having its throat cut off means you are blocking your expressiveness, even your natural breathing, a very destructive condition. You may be called to attend to the wisdom of your body more. Remember that dreams are about oneself but may be about the animal's condition too, so also reflect on the situation of the actual dog if it's your pet.

A man once had a dream that showed <u>a man's face turning into a dog's, and as it did so, he howled pleadingly. Ignored, he finally died.</u> Here the unconscious revealed a piteous cry behind the usual mask. Everyone has such a cry of longing, a longing for help, for sympathy, for satisfaction. A dog howls with his whole body. Out of his skin, bones, and beating heart he whines, moans, pleads for attention and care. The dog pleads for himself, echoing the cry in ourselves.

While dogs have been associated with the open strength of masculinity, cats suggest more of the hidden mysteries of femininity. Is there a connection to the fact that more cats suffer malicious cruelties than dogs?

A woman dreamed that <u>a man she desires runs over her cat with a car.</u> This woman's eroticism, purring warmth and sexual receptivity toward this man are painfully crushed. The man she loves had told her that he no longer wants to be with her. The dream is a dire warning that she must rescue this cat and not let it be killed because of his attitude. She must take extra precautions to protect her valuable feminine qualities.

The cat hunches her back, hisses, and claws. This seems a deceptively simple image. If it appears in regard to another person, you can sense how defensive you feel toward that person. The dream could be warning you of that person's mean intentions. It behooves you to be as hostile as a cat in unfavorable situations. Another option lies in how the moods of both men and women, which can be cozy and comfortable until they get jealous and resentful about not getting what they want, change and they suddenly attack. You may need to think about your needs and how to fulfill them more.

On the other hand, if your image shows the cat struggling against you, then you must ask yourself how are you trying to control your feline qualities? A cat will wrestle with you if you try to hold it down or block its freedom in any way. It knows and goes after what it wants. In what ways could you be hindering your independence or freedom of action in your life? Let your cat loose. See what it would take to turn it into a softer, gentler, purring creature.

Cats have never sold their souls to humans the way dogs did. They know their own minds, will not be coerced, and are very true to themselves in a way many of us lack.

The cat's independence remains its most coveted trait. Yet isn't it curious that every quality people love in cats they don't want in their partners—willfulness, the way they won't come when called, stay out all night, and sleep a lot? Couples prefer the qualities of dogs—loyalty and dependability.

We receive such precious gifts from animals. The famous cancer doctor, Dr. Bernie Siegel, says that he looks to dogs for inspiration on how to behave with unconditional love and spontaneity. And Linda Tellington-Jones, who does massage and acupressure on pets to calm their insecurities and anxieties and pains, says that when we open our hearts, we see their fear, aggression, fight, flight or freeze reactions and begin to see these reflected in ourselves. When we can do this, we feel identified with all creation.

Kanga Price, a woman I interviewed, suffered from many anxieties. In her fear and panic she felt alienated from her body and its painful reactions. Working with wounded animals led her to an acceptance of her body and greater spiritual wholeness. I'll end this section with some of her words.

> People are afraid of their animal selves. I had to embrace my animal, instinctual self in order to make a leap into a spirituality that made sense. We always try to separate our bodies from our spiritual being. If we hate our body/self, we lose touch with a courageous, exciting part of ourselves. If you hate a part of yourself, you cannot be spiritual…From animals I learn how to be 'in the now'. They are constantly in the 'present,' always alert to what is going on around them. With them you know exactly where you stand. There are no hidden agendas. They also relax and enjoy themselves. When they are hurt, they don't freak out; they get calm and try to rest. They are very clear about their boundaries, teach a respect for making space. They show pleasure and curiosity. They do not indulge in cynicism or self-pity nor do they get disillusioned or give up. They give so much and ask so little. They make me feel very connected to life and my Higher Power and universal love.

CONCLUSION

A Community for All Beings

The foregoing dip into the universe of animals has highlighted species of diverse talents and habitats in this current world. Because our future depends on these animals, they belong at the community table, treated as part of a democracy with rights.

Albert Einstein warned about this necessity:

A human being is part of the whole, called by us the Universe, a part limited in time and space. He experiences himself, his thoughts and feelings as something separate from the rest—a kind of optical delusion of his consciousness. The delusion is a kind of prison for us, restricting us to our personal desires and to affection for a few persons nearest to us. Our task must be to free ourselves from this prison by widening our circle of compassion to embrace all living creatures and the whole of nature in its beauty. Nobody is able to achieve this completely, but the striving for such achievement is in itself a part of the liberation and a foundation for inner security.[93]

When Walt Whitman wrote "I am the multitude," he recognized that each individual has the capacity to encompass other beings. And as animal imagery therapist Stephen Gallegos said, "The interior fauna reveal a realm of dynamic animal mediators who both embody and represent that which is otherwise obscure to the conscious self. They confirm the self as a community of being. We are so much larger than just Homo Sapiens."

---

93. *New York Post* (November 28, 1972).

We will not save what we do not love. Restorative efforts within community have proven to make people feel strong bonds of loyalty, akin to falling in love, not only to the animals, but to life and hope that carries them through difficult times.

To extend the boundaries of our sense of community to include all animal species then is both a practical and ethical step. First, the cost of restoring threatened wildlife is so much greater than just protection. Losing the genetic library of diversity puts the world into bankruptcy. The smartest move we, who have prided ourselves on our intelligence, could make is to include animals in our concerns. As Frans de Waal wrote, "Conscious community concern is at the heart of human morality."

In seeing ourselves as part of the circle of all beings, we acknowledge that animals bear the burdens we inflict upon them, and we are afflicted by their afflictions. We see that there is an "I" to whom I am responsible, and that my "I" is different from other human "I"'s as well as individual bear "I"'s and cow "I"'s. We don't have to project our interpretations onto others, nor deny their realities. We can consider the needs of all. I repeat, being useful to this larger community may very well fulfill our mysterious yearnings to belong.

It's not easy to be responsible to the animal community. We tend to drown (go unconscious) under everyday pressures. We get distracted from heeding the warning signs. News on television, radio, or newspapers doesn't help, for often information about wildlife is bypassed or not framed in an understandable way. Disastrous events go in one ear and out the other.

Scientists in the past contributed to the denigration of animals by referring to them with impersonal pronouns and in the passive voice. Such a canon was adopted because scientists had not found ways to measure animals' sensibilities and thus they just wouldn't acknowledge them. Researchers were made to use "instinct" for intelligence, "reflex" for mind. Recognizing that such rigid thinking is bad science and produces inaccurate hypotheses about emotion and intelligence, most contemporary scientists are finding different ways to construct their studies on the needs, thoughts, and feelings of species different from our own. Just as human psychology is studied, so is the psychology of other animals. We are co-evolving together in the current world.

Still even though scientists know that we are living organisms on a continuum with other organisms, they are slow to make moral and political declarations that would influence public policy decisions. A vision for a whole community of species requires the collaboration of scientists, legislators, farmers, all of us as we go about our work.

We may have to face inner prejudices. Just as we are known for racist and sexist attitudes in our treatment of each other, so we have "speciest" attitudes of superiority over other species. Other animals demonstrate abilities that are superior to Homo Sapiens—e.g. in sight, hearing, swimming, flying. The only reason human qualities are considered superior is that humans say so. (Likewise, men claim the right to beat their wives in many cultures and whites enslaved blacks).

The presumption of superiority not only excludes others, it's also spurious. Intelligence is not a guarantee of survival (recall the example of insects). Other animals do not destroy habitat or pollute the environment as our species has. If we judged species by which was most useful—made the most contributions—to Earth, where do you suppose we would rank?

We also get separated from natural plants and animals, the more accustomed to artificial things we get. Cars, bulldozers, trains, and miles of ugly shopping centers numb us to our surroundings. We see more buildings than forests. While some of us rave about man-made edifices, we've also become immune to much degradation in our lives.

The less we are aware of nature—and how we are part of it—the more diminished is our experience. Loss of contact with wildlife sets in motion apathy, disaffection, and carelessness. Feelings of hopelessness take over. Despairing people become passive and abusive. When probed, they reveal enormous grief and anger at their world. Abusive people are tormented by powerlessness, and when they behave cruelly, they are even more tormented by self-hate, which may well be disguised by increasing acts of violence to feel momentary relief from their powerlessness. Such entrapped people cannot care for themselves or others, much less other animals. These are the ones who kick or abandon dogs and cats, who drive along roads with rifles handy for shooting animals at whim.

Cruelty to oneself and others is the end-product of persistent feelings of alienation and separation from others. The death of our spirit is closely aligned to the death of species in our community.

In contrast, those who fulfill their hunger for nature in all its fierceness and joy have found that animals restore their passion and for life. Charles Darwin, himself a man of both science and religion, believed in our moral ability to care about other species and had reverence for the continuity of life. The path of passion is available to all. Remarkable results have come from people who have pursued it. They become healers themselves.

Scientist Barbara McClintock, who won a Nobel Prize in her 90's for her work with flies, felt affection, kinship and empathy for her subjects. Mary Batten, also a scientist and author of *Sexual Strategies* describes a typical numinous experience:

> One afternoon while sitting on a mountaintop on Panama's Barro Colorado Island, where the Smithsonian Tropical Research Institute maintains a field station, I felt strangely at home...free in some profound way. In this place, in the midst of such rich diversity, I sensed that the limitations of the human world and the intellectual barriers we erect between ourselves and the rest of nature were very small, almost insignificant—a humbling experience and, at the same time, quite joyful. At that moment I felt my personal identity expand beyond family, friends, nation, gender, and even species. I knew I was part of the grand continuum of life.[94]

Imagine if we carried this feeling into the political arena. Building alliances with animals is hardly the province of the scholarly. Plenty of ordinary citizens, including children, do it too. A woman in Florida was so fascinated with the swallow-tailed kites who lived around her that she became a fierce advocate when their habitat was ruined. She said she

---

94.   Mary Batten, *Sexual Strategies* (New York: Tarcher/Putnam, 1992), pp. xvi-xvii.

thought she just admired the birds but understanding their lives led her to learn more about the natural history of S. Florida, and then to scrutinize how she lived, the size of her house, the food she ate, the things she bought, and how she traveled around. She internalized the connections between the birds, her community, and other habits of her life.

Another example is how G. Sherman Morrison, an organizer for the N.American Coalition on Religion and Ecology, derived a philosophy of his own:

> I began with my own map with a dot to represent the Divine immanent within me. Around that dot I drew a small circle (a wonderful symbol of unity), to represent myself, and called it the psychological realm of existence. It is here that I explore the interrelationship of my mind, body, soul and spirit, and try to harmonize these different aspects of myself. I drew another circle around the first to recognize how my own existence is embedded within a context of other human beings. I therefore explore my relationship to my family, friends, the neighborhood in which I live, and the religious community of which I am a part.
>
> I added another ring around the first two and called it the ecological realm of existence. Reflecting on this, I recognize that my own life and the lives of all men and women, are dependent upon healthy ecosystems, which include not only plants and animals, but also soil, rocks, water, air, and energy.
>
> Finally I added one more concentric circle around all the others and called it the realm of Divine transcendence. I had begun with the Divine as immanent in my own soul, at the very core of individual existence. As the outermost circle, the Divine is also transcendent, greater than all that exists, encompassing all that exists. The individual, human society, and all of nature lie within the scope of the transcendent Divine, but are also infused with the immanent presence of God.
>
> It is this simple map of four concentric circles which I continually use to find my way. It helps me recognize where I am

and to account for everything to which I am related. The circles remind me of the need to be aware of the harmonious unity between these seemingly disparate aspects of life and to recognize that each aspect is embedded within and related to the others.

I believe that each of us is using a map—often unconsciously—on our daily journeys. How do we find the way that feels right to us in taking action steps? First, notice what animals appear most to you in dreams or your thoughts or experiences. You could begin with one who most intrigues or frightens you. Choosing just one may help to overcome being daunted by the need to preserve all species. Observe that animal in its habitat, if possible. Get a feel for its needs, features, style. Make entries in a journal about what strikes you as important. (See many more ideas in the final chapter).

You'll soon encounter current management policies on private and public land, water realms, in national parks, zoos, and laboratories. As you get familiar with some of the problems, put yourself into the position of the animals who live there.

Granted, the problems are complex. There are also differing perspectives among ourselves that add conflict. In resolving the difficulties and those that lie ahead, it may help to keep in mind Jung's assertion that only by enduring the tension of opposing views can we come to a transcendent perspective of the matters at hand.

Ideally wild animals would live freely on sufficient terrain for their populations to thrive. The more managers use darts, drugs, helicopters, pulleys, traps, radio collars, and snowmobiles to chase down animals and move them around fragmented areas, the more animals are robbed of their independence. The more we intervene, the more responsibility we assume. Some say we must to study the lives of animals so that we can provide better for them in the future. We have to make sure though that our methods permit animals to live with integrity.

The debate over managing wildlife reflects how we treat our bodies. Some avoid doctors and let "nature" take its course. That is the way some believe wilderness and animal populations should be treated. Some rush to the doctor every time they even suspect they have a symptom of a disease and dose themselves with medications. Similarly, some people want to micro-manage the changes in ecosystems. The moderate position lies in between: preventive measures and treatment when things get bad.

A difficult question is deciding just what level of abundance for wildlife species can be attained? Should our conservation goal be the way it was when the Indians prevailed? The journals of the early European explorers show that then in the west, for instance, there were 60–75 million bison, 30–40 million pronghorns, 10 million elk, 1.5–2 million sheep. In California grizzly bear sightings were 30–40 a day. Salmon runs were dense. Prairie dog towns were believed to hold 400 million.[95] In the last 300 years the wildlife count has obviously lessened. Now our task is to cling to the land fragments left before they are all gone and to connect as many as possible so that animals have safe roadless corridors.

The 1973 Endangered Species Act was once considered a milestone in the conservation of imperiled species. For updates on status, see www.endangered.fws.gov. The Act expired in 1993 and has yet to be reauthorized, largely due to political conflicts. In a testimony before Congress on behalf of the Act, Brock Evans emphasized how it's not a matter of choosing between species or people, because the future security of our planet, our health, our livelihoods, and our food supply depend on having a wealth of biological diversity.

Since the most imperiled species live on privately owned land, the government has endeavored to offer incentives to make landowners more cooperative. Historically such landowners own most of the land in this country but finance least of the conservation activity. A Cornell University study shows that five per-cent of landowners, including corporations, own three quarters of our privately-held land, and that this ownership is steadily being more monopolized by wealthy individuals and corporations, the leaders of which answer to no one.[96] Public lands, technically owned by all taxpayers, are managed by federal and state agencies that have the typical problems of large bureaucracies.

---

95. Dan Flores, *High Country News* (Colorado: August 18, 1997).

96. "This Land is My Land," *U.S. News & World Report* (New York: March 3, 1994).

After the costly court battles over the attempt to save the endangered Spotted Owl's habitat in old-growth forests, the idea emerged to save more species overall by protecting healthy and diverse ecosystems. The Clinton administration's contribution to the savings of species was to establish "habitat conservation plans." The deal was that landowners could destroy some habitat and even endangered species thereon as long as they do not harm or destroy too much and mitigate the losses elsewhere at their expense. Property owners got to have a "no surprises" guarantee, meaning that the government would not place further restrictions on how the land was used during the plan's life, usually several decades. Landowners were also to be paid for their protective measures.

Currently the under-funded and under-staffed federal agencies cannot keep up with the backlog or respond quickly to crisis situations. Nor will they go against the will of landowners. They also must satisfy demands for "multiple use" of lands and provide for recreation and hunting. However, if we insisted that our national priority was to preserve the community for all animals, then the agencies would have a clear mandate to live up to.

Laws are supposed to prevent greedy persons or companies or states from deliberately decimating an entire species. The threat of legal action motivates people but the procedures often result in delays, during which time animals are lost. Often if a rancher, farmer, or urbanite doesn't want a wild animal on their property, all s/he has to do is (illegally) "shoot, shovel, and shut up" or call the (federal) Animal Damage Control Agency, now sanitized into the "Wildlife Services," to remove the critter. Public taxpayer money is thus spent to kill wolves, coyotes, bears, mountain lions, fox, mice, beetles, blackbirds, deer, prairie dogs, etc. just because people consider them an obstacle to their plans.

On another front, we have relegated a number of our fellow travelers to national parks, zoos, and labs. Parks are large, zoos are smaller, and labs more confined still. How can we be useful and more sensitive to these inmates?

Our national parks are in danger of becoming fragmented islands, reserves surrounded by dense towns or cities for humans. Designed for tourists, they have steady streams of traffic and centers for food and gifts.

Managers of our 54 parks, which embrace 80 million acres and attract more than 250 million people annually, find themselves constantly torn between providing for the perpetuity of wildlife and the enjoyment of visitors. Snowmobiles attract winter tourists; yet the noise and fumes injure wildlife and disturb those seeking silence. While the beautiful lands are precious havens for wildlife, they also receive constant wear and tear.

Also since animals in the national parks don't know our rules, if they go beyond the park's boundary, they are likely to be shot. They are buzzed by sight-seeing airplanes and approached by camera-toting tourists. Food-flavored plastic wrap and aluminum foil clog their digestive systems. In a community of respect, these practices would be stopped.

How useful are zoos in our expanded community? Supporters argue that zoos can show people what wild animals look like up close. There, rare animals can be assisted in breeding with the potential of reintroducing offspring back into the wild. Zoos may be the last stop for imperiled species. But their educational function is pretty dull. Seeing caged animals also reinforces attitudes of our mastery over them. Caged animals have regular meals but little zest for life. With the need to hunt or fight taken away from them, their wits obsolesce. They have no escape.

Some say in circuses tigers and lions at least have a job to do.

The worst place for animals though is their imprisonment in experimental research laboratories. Proponents invoke the noble cause of curing disease in justifying their use of animals in this way. One wonders if the animals themselves are ever helped with the medicines for which they are forced to test? In a concerned community they would be.

So far we have lacked the moral strength to put an end to cruel practices. The experiences of Roger Fouts, who wrote *Next of Kin*, are relevant to this point. Roger Fouts showed how intertwined his personal life became with the status of research done with chimpanzees. For instance, he like many other scientists, depended on getting federal grants to carry on their careers. When President Reagan diverted all available funds to using chimps in bio-medical laboratories, Fouts' work on their abilities to communicate with sign language was stymied. Miserable over the loss of his chimp friends to medical research, Fouts turned to raising his own money for his research.

He and Jane Goodall, to the displeasure of the National Institute for Health, advocated that chimps be kept in groups, in large cages to allow exercise and socializing, infants be kept with their mothers, and their lives enriched with toys and activities. They joined a suit with the Animal Legal Defense Fund and Animal Welfare Institute against the failure of biomedical regs to uphold the Animal Welfare Act. The judge ruled in their favor but they later lost the case in appeal. The battle goes on.

The Animal Welfare Act is the federal law that governs the human care, handling, and treatment of animals in laboratories. Begun in 1966, its provisions do not prohibit any experiment, no matter how painful or useless; they simply set minimum housing and maintenance standards for confined animals. While covering those who sell to labs and intermediate handlers, dog and cat breeders, zoos, circuses, roadside menageries and transporters, they specifically exclude retail pet stores, county fairs, rodeos, purebred dog and cat shows. They cover dogs, cats, primates, or other warm-blooded animals used for research, testing or exhibition but not animals used for food or fiber. Horses are covered if used in experiments but not in entertainment events such as rodeos. The Act also excludes cold-blooded animals, such as turtles and snakes.

The Act uses only general terms for space requirements—that which allows "each animal to make normal postural and social adjustments with adequate freedom of movement." The Act does specifically govern an experiment but allows the withholding of anesthetics when ever "scientifically necessary." Periodic inspection of labs is supposed to take place, but is poorly enforced, nor is there any guarantee that a person from a humane organization will be included.

Is it right to kill other animals to prolong human life? How does killing affect our psyche? Must we inflict suffering on one species to relieve suffering in another? These are fundamental issues to be faced in establishing an ethical community.

Roger Fouts is an example of a professional who is not against medical research, but is for reducing the pain and suffering of lab animals and using alternatives to animal subjects when possible. His words and experience testify to his consciousness of other species:

> Compassion should not stop at the imagined barriers between species. Something is wrong with a system that exempts people from anticruelty laws just because those people happen to be wearing white lab coats. Science that dissociates itself from the pain of others soon becomes monstrous. Good science must be conducted with the head *and* the heart. Biomedical doctors have strayed too far from the guiding principle of the Hippocratic oath, "First, do no harm." Hippocrates was not referring only to humans. "The soul is the same in all living creatures," he said, "although the body of each is different."[97]

Recognizing that animals need more protections and rights, within the last ten years for the first time in history some law schools, including Harvard and Georgetown, offer courses in animal law. A scholarly journal, *Animal Law*, is published. Animal lawyers, seeking to elevate the status of animals beyond that of property, have won some victories. In the near future they say watch for testimony in court by an intelligent chimp or gorilla.

While we might agree philosophically that every living being in nature has an inalienable right to food, space, freedom, we are unwilling to say just how much when we clash over the same food, space, and right to be free. Currently, it is possible for us to decide what animals should or should not live—a terribly dangerous power. We can abolish mosquitoes because they annoy or carry malaria even though many animals eat them for food and they may have other functions beyond our ken. When we approach the dilemma of how to respond to a species that we perceive as a threat, we can assess the risk and find options, other than extermination. For instance, medication protects people from malaria. Just because deer pass Lyme disease to humans, the majority of people do not favor eradication but are looking for other protections. When resources are tight

---

97.   Roger Fouts, *Next of Kin* (New York: William Morrow, 1997), p. 371.

and we compete with other animals for them, instead of just exerting our prerogative, planning for shared use is possible. We can be more creative about meeting needs. Some would assign a monetary value to species but the trouble with that idea is the assumption that we can own and barter nature, which is a fallacy. Nature owns us, no matter how much we try to possess her creations.

Roderick Nash in *The Rights of Nature/A History of Environmental Ethics* described the slow progress toward the recognition that nature has moral standing worth federal protection. He points out that in our country American colonists first declared their right of freedom from the British in the Declaration of Independence (1776). Slaves were granted their right of freedom in the Emancipation Proclamation (1863). In the 19th century women won the right to vote. (An Equal Rights Amendment for women has not as yet been passed.) Native Americans won rights under our governmental rule in the Indian Citizenship Act (1924). Blacks won Civil Rights in 1957. Protection for endangered species came in 1973.

Groups come at the issue of rights from different directions, and so we need patience with the ironies. For instance, while people kill millions of animals for food annually, conservationists tend to ignore factory-farming issues. The Humane Society, while lobbying for better treatment of animals, euthanizes huge numbers to end suffering. Conservationists tend to focus more on populations and ecosystems; rightists on individuals and farm and lab animals.

We can't depend on all the welfare or conservation organizations to protect every species. Nor is halting the raising of animals for food or research the answer. In the end Aldo Leopold's most famous maxim matters most: "a thing's right when it tends to preserve the integrity, stability and beauty of the biotic community. It is wrong when it tends otherwise."[98]

Religions have historically supported ethical respect for animals and the whole of creation. Nevertheless, Western religions tend to justify harm to animals for economic reasons (food, medicine, property), while Eastern

---

98. Aldo Leopold, *Sand County Almanac* (New York: Oxford University Press, 1949), pp. 224-5).

religions, despite their emphasis on non-duality, let animals suffer by neglecting their health and welfare. Feelings of kinship with all of creation for many is a spiritual experience that arises out of ecological facts. Those who hold to the unity of self and other created beings want to commune with animals and nature. On the other hand, in case after case it's been proven that those who maintain attitudes of separation also lack care and compassion for animals.

Feeling a covenant with butterflies, cats, whales, and humans becomes a spiritual process, a walk with the divine. It involves being able to contain your ego's (limited) impulses to control or flee when confronted with strangeness or challenge. A good way to start is to count the blessings of nature, to feel gratitude for the animals. Have a heart that listens to animals.

Sensitivity to the beauty of animals would be the best result of becoming more informed about them. Facts produce wisdom, nourished by awakened senses and feelings. The use of our imaginations—the capacity to image (often inspired by dreams)—is possibly our greatest asset. The evolution of world cultures has been less influenced by government leaders than the ideas of ordinary people. Futures must be envisioned and spoken. If you commit to yours, the power opens doors you could not have foreseen.

I especially encourage immersion in nature's beautiful places so that you can be inspired by the grace and variety of thriving animals. Beauty can lead us to love our kin on the Earth rather than genetic engineering, virtual realities, or colonies in space. A stimulated imagination, inspired by wisdom and wonder about animals, creates an excellent basis for setting our priorities. If we remember who we really are in the family of life, we have a chance to bring much-needed empathy for animals into our political, economic, scientific, religious, and educational systems.

The future is open. May we approach it with all our laments and outrage over the current state of our lives and that of animals. From tussling with the issues, may a deluge of insights and images emerge from the ecological unconscious, in continuous waves that underscore the unity of being.

How to Work with Animals in I-Thou Relationship

This chapter contains exercises that facilitate a stronger inner relationship between you and other animals. You may follow these suggested practices as you read chapters of the book or you may use them as a reference from time to time. Engaging in these exercises will greatly extend your sensitivity to animals and your understanding of their role in your life and your role in theirs.

Relationship with other humans has taught us that we are more likely to avoid conflict if we know them well, including why they hold certain positions and values. Seeing the other as distinct from our self—walking on their path—is the basis for good communication. So it is with other animals.

Research

The first step is to learn about your chosen animal(s). The references and books in the Selected Reading list are good places to start. (Going to conferences can give you scientific and political background, as well as a network of friends.) Field guides are excellent for learning about the physical features and survival needs of any animal. For cultural myths, *The Golden Bough* is a classic. Other encyclopedias, such as those edited by Mircea Eliade or Joseph Campbell, about the archetypal meaning of animal in myths, symbols, or rituals are worth consulting. Furthermore, you may be led to study the major religious texts: the Bible, Upanishads, Koran, or African, Egyptian, Celtic lore. The art of cultures may appeal to you. Keep in mind that the many names for God—Allah, Higher Power,

Being/Nonbeing—are just metaphors for that which transcends all, and mythology can be used to maintain wonder in the mystery of the universe and to provide instruction in meeting life's difficulties.

If you treat research like a detective solves a mystery, you will find this an exciting part of your life's journey. For, you are on a quest. You are searching for the holy grail to heal that which ails you and the world. Many fairy tales start with something wrong in the kingdom; doom and gloom lie all around. You are about to play the part of the hero who faces challenges to bring joy and health back to the kingdom.

On your journey the world participates with you and your efforts. Through encounters—whether physical, imaginative, or dreamlike—the world speaks to you and you respond, because your psyche is rooted in nature, ever dynamic and changing. Being human means being at one with our landscape, including the animals native to it.

To heighten your awareness of which animals are important to you, go where you may see them and spend time simply observing. How do they sound, smell, feel to the touch? What is their condition in the community? What emotions do you have in their presence?

In private try behaving like a chosen animal in its habitat, whether in forest, water, cage. Feel into its body. Although knowing the animals are independent beings, let the boundaries blur as you imagine your way into the life of the animal as it goes through a typical day, alert to its desires, struggles, and dangers. Feel the connections between your ways and theirs. Letting its being infuse you for a time helps sensitize you to an animal's outer life as well as to its potential within you as a guide.

Meditation

An approach for discovering which animals are of importance to your life is found by doing the following meditation. (Other methods of "journeying" may be found in the works of Stephen Gallegos and Michael Harner.)

As in all meditations, the first step is to find a quiet place. Sit down with your hands rested in your lap. Permit yourself to relax and detach from the concerns of your day. You may also lie down as long as there is no danger of your falling asleep. Close your eyes and follow your breathing. If you desire, you may set an intention, such as healing an emotional wound from the past or resolving a current conflict.

Focus on your toes and notice how they feel. Sense the energy flow in the balls of your feet, then your ankles, and calves. Slowly move up the length of your body, focusing your awareness on as many parts as you can: knees, thighs, buttocks, genitals, abdomen, lungs, chest, heart, arms, elbows, wrists, fingers, shoulders, neck, head, ears, eyes, mouth, jaw, nose, to the top of your head. Taking time to quiet your mind and body is an excellent prelude to deeper work.

Then call upon the animal that you need to help with the problem to appear. Choose either a favorite or let your imagination send forth the appropriate one. Spontaneity allows more room for the unconscious to participate. Letting whatever animal emerge means that this animal is personal and relevant to you. The appearance of a certain animal means both that it would like something of you and has something to give. You may commune about these questions in your meditation.

Afterward, to keep the animal alive in your psyche, write or draw or dance your experiences. At other times contact it again in a meditation. Notice which animals appear to you frequently. Take notes on the animals' behavior and wisdom over time. As you befriend an animal, a bond intensifies. Animal appearances have a life of their own, showing up over decades and illuminating different situations. The more you know your animals, the more they will have to show you.

There are many reasons for connecting with animals in such meditations: feeling dispirited, fearful, demoralized, sick, depressed. Contact with animals has the benefit of enlivening one, sharpening your focus, making you more direct and assertive, clarifying your intentions. When you feel weak, this kind of meditation is a way to get your power back.

Journal Techniques

These guidelines offer you a structured, safe, comprehensive way of working with your thoughts, feelings, and dreams in relation to animals.

They are adapted from many years of using and teaching of Ira Progoff's Intensive Journal Method.

The actual journal you use can be a spiral notebook or handmade paper bound in leather, whatever you like. However, I recommend a loose-leaf notebook because it has the advantage of being able to be divided into sections, to which you can add over time. Your journal can be as expansive as you want it—after all, it is your creation and tool. Don't hesitate to add drawings or photos. Make room for each of the following sections.

Daily Log: In this section describe your research results and notable encounters with actual animals. If you are struck by a documentary or magazine article or book, describe your thoughts here. Record the feelings evoked by material in this book. This section may also be used as a repository for anything that the following sections don't include.

Meditation Log: Here record the results of your meditations. Keeping them collected in one place will make them easier to refer back to. It is very helpful to have easy access to these inner experiences.

Memory Log: From time to time it's worthwhile going back over your life to recall your experiences with and attitudes toward animals in the past. Follow these steps:

Divide your life into about ten main periods, beginning with early childhood and ending with the present. After identifying these periods, go back into each one and write briefly about your relationship to animals at that time. Perhaps you had a beloved pet. Maybe for school you raised tadpoles and frogs. Did you go into the woods and see animals or notice the birds and fish around a beach? As you matured, what were your attitudes toward animals? Perhaps you became a member of a conservation organization or went on a wildlife-viewing vacation?

More elaborately describe a specific memory with an animal. Was there a moment that you treasured? Perhaps the cuddling of a dog or cat or the grief you felt at the death of a pet. Or, an encounter with a wild animal.

Dream Log: Here you will maintain a chronological record of your dreams. To remember your dreams, leave a pad by your bed at night, and when you wake up after a dream, write down what you can recall. (You can do this in the dark, even half-asleep).

Dream Enlargements: Keep a separate section for your additional work on dreams. Because dreams can sometime seem mystifying, you may give up trying to understand them. More important than figuring them out is simply turning the images over in your mind during your day. A dream usually has a story. First, the setting is introduced, then the problem. Actions ensue that arouse strong feelings. Some dreams seem like theatrical presentations; these often are archetypal and pack a powerful punch.

At first notice where in your body you feel the dream. See if you can identify with what the animal is doing. Focus on the expression in the eyes and let yourself be absorbed by the energy there. Ask what is it like to be in the animal's body and to see this way. Transferring into the animal's perspective can help you move into the atmosphere of the dream. Ask what in your life the dream is referring to.

Taking advantage of the material I offer in this book, follow the lead of the dream to look up more information about an animal's behavior and needs, as well as its mythology or symbolic values in the art and religion of different cultures. Some dream writers assign definite meanings to animals, but this approach is too rigid and restrictive. It is much better to notice the meanings that resonate most forcefully within you.

That said, here are some typical themes and guidelines. If you have long been estranged from your psyche, animals often appear hostile, even raging at you. But these animals can be befriended. When an animal chases a person in a dream, this indicates that a particular instinct has been split off and needs to be integrated. Suppressed instincts are the dangers, not the animals. Disregarding our instincts leads to frightening nightmares as the unconscious tries to get our attention. Nightmares scare our egos but if we shut our minds to them, an even worse nightmare returns.

On the other hand, when an animal is met and respected in your psyche, you know an unmatched power and calm. You become kinder and more empathetic. You feel fiercely connected to all of life. You want to preserve and protect the world.

A good rule of thumb is that if you feel negatively toward the deeper feelings of the unconscious, animals will appear dangerous and frightening. If the dreamer is in rapport with the psyche, animals will appear helpful or friendly.

In a typical dream someone may be trying to rescue a small dark animal that tends to stay hidden, is shy and wary. This person probably is also afraid to come out in the sunlight, to be seen, to frolic in the open. Both the person and the animal may be frightened in their journeys on Earth at this time.

Because most of us are wounded in relation to our animal selves, in dreams animals often appear injured in some crucial way. An animal crying for help should make you ask what basic need or instinct is being denied, suppressed, or ignored. Sunshine, contact with the soil, awareness of the phases of the moon and seasonal nuances (colors, foliage, temperatures) restore our vitality. We need to be in better tune with our need for certain foods, enough sleep, and our body's healing abilities.

Often animals appear as starved. Neglected too long, they need to be fed. Just as endangered animal species have been depleted by lack of living space and food, so over-domestication and development starve our souls. Too many of us live dreary lives doing our duties with just small doses of happiness. Like all animals, we want to flourish, not just survive. Symptoms of soul starvation include dryness, depression, confusion, fatigue, numbness, shame, cringing before authority, being overly nice, fear of change, having no time for yourself to muse and wander freely. When we fall victims of abusive people and organizations, losing the incentive to speak up and/or escape, we literally efface the integrity of our beings.

The most spiritually profound dreams and imaginative flights involve sexual union with animals. Such imagery should not be taken literally but as a symbolic representation of union between the dreamer's ego attitudes and the qualities of the animal. Copulation with a bear or a horse or a tiger unites the individual with the animal's special strengths. After long-lasting and thrilling fusions, a dreamer would feel substantially energized and fertilized. These are blessed moments.

The lover as animal often appears in literature, art, fantasy or any work of the imagination. One example is the Olmec people, who thrived over 1000 years B.C.E. in central America. They frequently made sculptures of women in sexual union with jaguars, which inspired their becoming known as the "Jaguar People." Another example is the legend of Leda and the Swan. Zeus assumed the form of a swan in order to seduce the mortal Leda, believing her to be more receptive to a swan than a god. It appears that he can only impregnate her with divinity through the form of an animal.

The animals that appear in your dreams are ones with whom you may choose to initiate a dialogue. Simply because they have appeared in your dreams means they have something of significance to teach you, and the meditative dialogue method may be the best way to get the messages revealed.

Dialogues: This section of the journal comprises the ongoing record of written dialogues you have with animals from time to time. As we get to know animals, recognizing that they are different from us but that we are part of the unity of being, empathy can flow between us increasingly. In the fluid "space between," we reach out from heart to heart in I-Thou relationship.[99]

After relaxing and meditating, sit with your journal open. Visualize yourself with an animal you knew in the past, one you'd like to know more about, one that you dreamed about, or one that you sense serves as a power (or numinous) animal for you. The main criterion should be

99.   Martin Buber, a Judaic philosopher, coined this phrase in *I and Thou*, tr. by Walter Kaufman (New York: Scribners, 1970).

that you feel you could open your heart to this animal or that you would like to have access to the kind of knowledge this animal represents. After you have selected your animal and with eyes closed, visualize yourself with it and start a dialogue. You speak to it and let it speak back to you. Let the dialogue unfold on paper as spontaneously as possible.

Until you get used to this mode of communication, simply greet the animal and go from there. Or, you may start with a question that has been preoccupying you. If you can't get going, describe your awkwardness. If you feel you are making it up, ask the animal to speak about its life or wishes in a dream. Listen for the animal's response. Remember, this is to be a dialogue, not a monologue.

This dialogue technique can stimulate deeper layers of conscious and unconscious knowledge, if done meditatively with awareness of the animal as Other. The knowledge that is activated dwells in the space between your ordinary awareness and that of the animal's.

You cannot attain satisfactory results by speaking your side only. When you just describe how you think or feel about a problem, you do what is most often done in diaries. You are expressing your limited perspective on things. The key to a dialogue is to introduce another intelligence. In that interaction you can be led to new insights. The deeper you go, the more your psyche can extend its boundaries and take in the perceptions of the other animal. That is why you don't want to write this dialogue as if in a play of your own direction but let it unfold in its own meandering, surprising way. Let the animals speak, and then assess the wisdom you gain.

*   *   *

Here is a brief excerpt from one of the dialogues a newly pregnant woman had with a tiger:

Susan: I felt your strength, your courage, and your roar inside me. Now I want to speak with you. What do you want to tell me?

Tiger: You have had me all along but you never knew it. You can feel the ripple of my muscles. You are always ready in an alertness that is nonetheless relaxed.

Susan: Ready, yes, but I don't see the courage yet.

Tiger: That you cannot see in yourself, but as you live inside me and manifest your power you will see it. It will begin to glow. And people will recognize the courage of the Large Cat Spirit and they will not mess with you.

Susan (seeing herself become the tiger lying in the sun and panting with a slack belly): Will I be fierce or tender as you?

Tiger: You can be the gentlest creature on the earth. Know me and feel the red courage line to the heart begin to grow strong, straight and glowing. You have a lot to do yet in this world. You will need this courage to keep you strong and at the ready. Now walk away with full padded paws and easy hips. Keep your ears and eyes alert. Trust the fire in your belly.

In this dialogue you can see how Susan integrated aspects of the tiger's energy, actually merging with her for awhile. She will reenter her life with the memory of the tiger. Then she will be able to call up the tiger when she is in a difficult situation. From time to time she will freshen her energy with the tiger's spirit. Keep in mind this excerpt is just an example from a dialogue. Dialogues follow no set patterns. Have no expectations and treat each one as a new experience.

An Indian chief once said:

If you talk to the animals, they will talk with you
And you will know each other.
If you do not talk to them, you will not know them
And what you do not know, you will fear
What one fears, one destroys.[100]

---

100. Rick McIntyre, *A Society of Wolves*. (Minnesota: Voyageur Press, 1996).

Action

As a result of this inner work, it is always important to ask: where does it lead me? The dreams, meditations or dialogues will apply to specific areas of your life, after which you should determine a specific action to take. An action could be to change your work or a relationship in some way, or to help save a threatened animal and habitat.

Honor your research and journal work by giving them quality time. Remember that you are giving love to yourself and your bond with the world when you do. If you do this inner work, there is no doubt that the core of your self will evolve and along with it your contribution to life on Earth. You have gifts to make to other beings but to do so seems to require the deep inner work that extends our boundaries to include all.

In learning about animals and reflecting on their relevance to your life, follow the trails that beckon even if their scent at first seems faint. Remember, doing these kinds of exercises was once the stuff of sacred mysteries. The greatest heroes incarnated themselves sequentially—as hare, fish, bird—in order to gain the wisdom of wild nature. So, in the spirit of a 19th century Gaelic blessing, may "Wisdom of serpent be thine, Wisdom of raven be thine,………………."

Selected Reading

Abt, Regina; Bosch, Irmgard; MacKrell, Vivienne. *Dream Child.* Switzerland: Daimon Verlag, 2000.

Ackerman, Diane. *The Rarest of the Rare, The Moon By Whale Light.* New York: Random House, 1989.

Ammer, Christine. *It's Raining Cats and Dogs.* New York: Paragon House, 1989.

Andrews, Ted. *Animal-Speak.* Minnesota: Llewellyn Publications, 1996.

Angier, Natalie. *The Beauty of the Beastly.* Boston: Houghton Mifflin, 1995.

Bass, Rick. *The Ninemile Wolves.* New York: Ballantine, 1993.

Mary Batten, *Sexual Strategies.* New York: Tarcher/Putnam, 1992.

Boone, J. Allen, *Kinship of All Life.* San Francisco: HarperSanFrancisco, 1954.

Brazaitis, P. & Watanabe, M. (ed). *The Fight for Survival, Animals in their Natural Habitats.*, New York: Friedman Group, 1994.

Budiansky, Stephen. *The Nature of Horses.* New York: The Free Press, 1997.

Burger, Carl. *All About Fish.* New York: Random House, 1960.

Busch, Robert H. *The Wolf Almanac.* New York, Lyons & Burford, 1995.

Byatt, A.S.. *Morpho Eugenia.* New York: Random House, 1992.

Caras, Roger. *A Perfect Harmony.* New York: Simon & Schuster, 1996.

Carr Archie. *Handbook of Turtles.* New York: Cornell University Press, 1952.

Caspari, Elizabeth with Ken Robbins. *Animal Life in Nature, Myth and Dreams.* Illinois: Chiron Publications, 2003.

Dooling, D.M., trans. *The Bestiary of Christ.* New York: Parabola Books, 1991.

Eisner, Thomas. *For Love of Insects.* Cambridge, Mass.: The Belknap Press, 2003.

Eldridge, Niles. *Life in the Balance, Humanity and the Biodiversity Crisis.* Princeton: Princeton University Press, 1998.

An Encyclopedia of Archetypal Symbolism. Vol. 1, ed. by Beverly Moon, Vol. 2, ed. by George R. Elder. Boston: Shambhala, 1996, 1997.

Environmental Ethics (Journal.) Denton, TX: University of N. Texas.

Estes, Clarissa Pinkola *Women Who Run With the Wolves.* New York: Ballantine, 1992.

Ferguson, Gary. *The Yellowstone Wolves: The First Year.* Montana: Falcon Press, 1996.

Fouts, Roger. *Next of Kin.* New York: Wm. Morrow, 1997

Fischer-Screiber, I. *et al., The Rider Encyclopedia of Eastern Philosophy and Religion.* London: Rider, 1998.

Frazer, Sir James George. *The Golden Bough.* New York: Macmillan, 1995.

Gallegos, Stephen. *Animals of the Four Windows.* Santa Fe: Moon Bear Press, 1991.

Gore, Al. *Earth in the Balance.* Boston: Houghton Miflin, 1992.

Greene, Harry W. *Snakes.* California: U of California Press, 1997.

Hall, Nor. *The Moon and the Virgin.* New York: Harper & Row, 1980.

Harrison, Jim. *The Theory and Practice of Rivers,* 1989*; Just Before Dark,* 1991. Montana: Clark City Press.

Harte, John. *The Green Fuse.* California: U of California Press, 1993.

Hearne, Vicki. *Adam's Task.* New York: Vintage, 1987; *Animal Happiness.* New York: Harper Collins, 1994.

Heinrich, Bernd. *Mind of the Raven.* New York: Harper Collins, 1999.

Hoage, R.J. (ed). *Perceptions of Animals In American Culture.* Washington, D.C.: Smithsonian Institution Press, 1989.

Hogan, Linda. *Dwellings.* New York: Simon & Schuster, 1995.

Hubbell, Sue. *Broadsides From the Other Orders.* New York: Random House, 1993; *Waiting for Aphrodite (Journeys Into the Time Before Bones).* Boston: Houghton Miflin, 1999.

In the Company of Animals. New York: New School of Social Research, Vol.62(3), Fall 1995.

Intimate Nature, The Bond Between Women and Animals. Linda Hogan, Deena Metzer, Brenda Peterson (editors). New York: Fawcett Columbine, 1998.

Ives, Richard. *Of Tigers and Men.* New York: Doubleday, 1997.

Jacobi, Jolande; Jung, Carl (ed). *Man and His Symbols.* New York: Doubleday, 1964.

Johnson, Buffie. *Lady of the Beasts.* San Francisco: Harper & Row, 1988.

Kellert, Stephen. *The Value of Life.* Washington, D.C.: Island Press, 1996.

Kerasote, Ted. *Bloodties.* New York: Kodansha International, 1993.

Leopold, Aldo. *A Sand County Almanac.* New York: Oxford University Press, 1949.

Limerick, Patricia. *The Legacy of Conquest.* New York: W.W. Norton, 1987.

Lopez, Barry. *Of Wolves and Men.* New York: Scribner, 1978.

Masson, Jeffery. *When Elephants Weep; The Emperor's Embrace (Reflections on Animal Families and Fatherhood).* New York: Delacorte, 1995.

Matsen, Brad. *Planet Ocean.* California: Ten Speed Press, 1994.

Mech, David. *The Wolf: The Ecology and Behavior of an Endangered Species.* Minnesota: U of Minnesota Press, 1991.

Melson, Gail F.. *Why the Wild Things Are: Animals in the lives of children.* Cambridge: Harvard U Press, 2001.

Mery, Fernand. *The Life, History and Magic of the Cat.* New York: Madison Square Press, 1967.

Miller, G.Tyler. *Living in the Environment.* California: Wadsworth, 1992.

Monks of New Skete. *The Art of Raising a Puppy.* Boston: Little, Brown, 1991.

Morton, E. & Page, J.. *Animal Talk.* New York: Random House, 1992.

Nash, Roderick. *The Rights of Nature/A History of Environmental Ethics.* Wisconsin: U of Wisconsin Press, 1989.

Nelson, Richard. *Heart and Blood, Living with Deer in America.* New York: Knopf, 1997.

Noble, Vicki. *Shakti Woman.* New York: Harper San Francisco, 1991.

Peacock, Doug. *Grizzly Years.* New York: Holt, 1990.

Pluhar, Evelyn B.. *Beyond Prejudice, Moral Significance of Human and Nonhuman Animals.* North Carolina: Duke University, 1995.

Quammen, David. *The Song of the Dodo.* New York: Scribner, 1996.

Rezendes, Paul. *The Wild Within.* California: Tarcher/Putnam, 1998.

Rockwell, David. *Giving Voice To Bear.* Colorado: Rinehart, 1991.

Roszak, Theodore. *The Voice of the Earth.* New York: Simon & Schuster, 1992.

Safina, Carl. *Song for the Blue Ocean.* New York: Holt, 1998.

Saunders, Nicholas. *Animal Spirits.* Boston: Little, Brown, 1995.

Shepard, Paul. *The Others: How animals made us human.* Washington, D.C.: Island Press, 1996.

Steinhart, Peter. *The Company of Wolves.* New York: Knopf, 1995.

Swain, Roger. *Saving Graces: Sojurns of a Backyard Biologist.* Boston: Little, Brown, 1991

Thomas, Elizabeth Marshall. *The Tribe of Tiger.* New York: Simon & Schuster, 1994; *The Hidden Life of Dogs.* G. K. Hall, 1994.

Tobias, Michael, *Nature's Keepers, On the Front Lines of the Fight to Save Wildlife in America,* New Jersey: John Wiley, 1998.

Towery, Twyman. *The Wisdom of Wolves.* Illinois: Sourcebooks, 1997.

Van Der Post, Laurens. *About Blady.* New York: Wm. Morrow, 1991.

Walker, Barbara, *The Women's Encyclopedia of Myths and Secrets.* San Francisco: Harper & Row, 1983.

de Waal, Frans. *GOOD NATURED, The Origins of Right and Wrong in Humans and Other Animals.* Cambridge: Harvard University Press, 1996.

Whitfield, P.. *From So Simple a Beginning, The Book of Evolution.* New York: Macmillan, 1993.

Wilcove, David. *The Condor's Shadow: The Loss and Recovery of Wildlife in America*. New York: W. H. Freeman, 1999.

Wilson, E.O.. *The Diversity of Life*. Cambridge: The Belknap Press of Harvard University Press, 1992.

Yoerg, Sonja I.. *Clever As a Fox*. New York: Bloomsbury Publishing, 2001.

ACKNOWLEDGMENTS

My heartiest thanks go to the following individuals for their contributions to the creation of this book: Ann Mari Ronnberg of the Archive of Research in Archetypal Symbolism in New York's C.G. Jung Center, the founders and staff of Fundacion Valparaiso in Spain, Jean Naggar, Aurelie Sheehan, Jan Beyea, Jim Jacobs, Amy Zarrett, Joe Gutkoski, Sue Sabol, Barbara Link, John Platt, Tina DeWeese, Connie Myslik, Charles Kelly, Joan Bird, Tom Skeele, Todd Wilkinson, Dennis Flath, Ken Barrett, Jo Shields, Jo Flagg, Shaun Phoenix, Susan Ewing, Beverly Compton, Marilyn Davis, Kanga Price, Deborah Butterfield.

0-595-34311-2